YOU CAN
BET ON IT!

DEDICATION

I dedicate this book to all sports bettors. You get a certain, indefinable thrill when you place a wager on a sporting event: you almost become part of the action you are betting on. The highs and lows cannot be explained—they can only be felt.

The guest columnists have all ridden the wild horse of sports betting. And because they are intelligent and possess personal strengths, they have survived and thrived. I have a tremendous amount of respect for what they do and for who they are. I truly thank them for their contributions to this book.

I also thank my editor, Dana Smith, for her professionalism and guidance. Work places can indeed breed friendships.

For the past 15 years I have hosted *You Can Bet On It*, a Las Vegas radio show featuring sports handicappers, sports book directors, poker champions, and gaming authors. I want to thank all of the experts for sharing honest betting information with the public.

Since many of these chapters were first written, some guest writers have passed away. My life was enriched by their friendship and sports bettors everywhere are bettor off for their professionalism and wisdom.

Last, but certainly not least, I thank my family and friends for their support and inspiration. They mean more to me than they will ever know.

I wish you all the right bounces at all the right times, and may you all have many winning seasons.

Larry Grossman
September 2004

YOU CAN BET ON IT!

INSIDE SECRETS OF SPORTS BETTING
FROM THE MEN WHO SET THE LINE

by Larry Grossman

CARDOZA PUBLISHING

Cardoza Publishing is the foremost gaming publisher in the world, with a library of over 100 up-to-date and easy-to-read books and strategies. These authoritative works are written by the top experts in their fields and, with more than 7,500,000 books in print, represent the best-selling and most popular gaming books anywhere.

FIRST CARDOZA EDITION

Library of Congress Catalog Card No: 2004101404
ISBN: 1-58042-140-7

Visit our new web site (www.cardozapub.com)
or write us for a full list of books and computer strategies.

CARDOZA PUBLISHING
P.O. Box 1500, Cooper Station, New York, NY 10276
Phone (800)577-WINS
email: cardozapub@aol.com
www.cardozapub.com

TABLE OF CONTENTS

PUBLISHERS' INTRODUCTION............................9

1. INSIDE SECRETS: THE BETTING LINE
How the Lines Are Set....................................... 13
How the Lines Are Moved.................................16
The Real Story Behind the Lines.......................20
Shopping Sportsbooks for Value.......................23
Realistic Goals Against the Lines.....................26
Winning $100,000...30

2. MAKING MONEY: GENERAL WINNING CONCEPTS
30 Rules for Success..35
The ABC's of Sports Handicapping...................42
18 Frequent Mistakes in Sports Wagering.........58
Mike Lee's Handicapping Success Formula....................65
Put Yourself in the Position to Win...................70

3. PROFESSIONAL PLAYS
Betting Over/Unders...75
Betting Propositions...82
Betting Parlays...88

4. BEATING THE GAMES

Football
Element X..95
Getting an Extra Angle...97
Win with Patience...100
Tools of the Trade...102
Getting a Feel for the Action...............................105

Baseball
Picking Winners..107
Betting on the Run Line.......................................110
A Visit To Bad Beat City......................................116

Basketball
Betting College and Pro Basketball.....................120
The Scoop on Home Court Hoops........................124

Horseracing
The Horse Parlors of the 1940s............................129
Computers and Thoroughbred Handicapping........133
Exotic Bets..138
Dosage and the Kentucky Derby..........................140
Betting Maidens...143

NASCAR
Betting on NASCAR..147

Golf
Betting on Golf..155

5. INFORMATION YOU NEED TO WIN
Information...163
Misinformation..170
The Myth of the Lock..172

Handicapping with Computers.........................174
Integrity A.........................176
Integrity B.........................180

6. MONEY MANAGEMENT
The Dogs Were Barking.........................185
Money Management—My Opinion!.........................187
Realities of Beating the Bookie.........................191

7. PEOPLE IN THE GAME
Lem Banker.........................195
Sonny Reizner.........................198
Andrew Iskoe.........................203
Lou Kopple.........................207
Howard Schwartz.........................210
Mike Lee.........................212
About the Guest Columnists.........................215

PUBLISHERS'
INTRODUCTION

If you want to make money betting sports, you've come to the right place. In the following pages, you'll learn the inside secrets of how the lines are made, where to find the angles to beat them, and how to always get the best bang for your sports betting dollar, no matter what sport you bet on. If Vegas sets a line on it, we'll show you how to beat it—from football, baseball, basketball, and golf to horseracing, NASCAR, boxing, and more.

This book contains a wealth of valuable and profitable secrets to sports betting, contributed by the world's foremost sports betting specialists. And this is no ordinary group of experts—it's a who's who of sports handicappers. These are the men who set the lines you see in every newspaper in the country. They know more about beating the bookie than any group of men alive, and they should—in some cases, they are the bookie! Thanks to their proven strategies, sound advice, and money-making tips found in this book, you'll soon be betting and winning like a pro.

If you think there is one book you need to be a winner at sports betting, relax—you're holding that book in your hands right now.

-Avery Cardoza

CHAPTER

1

INSIDE SECRETS: THE BETTING LINE

1

How the Lines Are Set

by "Roxy" Roxborough
Former President, Las Vegas Sports Consultants

I'd rather have preparation than motivation. Everyone likes to play and no one likes to practice.

-- Bum Phillips

The Function of the Line

The line, or odds, is the key to running a successful sportsbook. The primary function of the line is to balance action. Linemakers are not concerned with splitting the opinions of all sports fans or even all sports bettors. Their concern is to attract equal amounts of money on each side of an event. Therefore, linemaking involves handicapping the bettors who create the bulk of the action.

Suppose the Giants are a 2-point favorite over the Saints and there are 101 bettors interested in the game. 100 of those like the Giants at -2 for $55 to win $50. The last bettor likes the Saints at +2 for $5,500 to win $5,000. The line certainly didn't split the opinions of the 101 bettors. However, it did split the money, which is the most any oddsmaker or bookmaker can ask.

The Basis of the Line

The foundation of the line is the opinions of bettors who create the majority of action. The linemaker predicts how these bettors will react to widely available information and arrives at a line. The sophistication of the clientele that bets a sport will determine how the linemaker interprets the information. In the NFL, long-standing reputations of teams are a large consideration because the majority of the action comes from people who do little statistical analysis.

The general factors that linemakers consider are talent, situational analysis, and public perception. Situational analysis is the study of special circumstances that affect team performance.

For example, a widely followed situation in professional sports is to bet against a baseball team the day after they clinch the division. There are literally hundreds of these situations that get attention, regardless of their profitability. In college sports, talent and public perception take precedence. Professional sports rely more on situational analysis.

The role of feedback in linemaking is remarkable. When the bettors vote with their dollars, they are either betting with a team or against a team. It becomes clear after a few games which teams the bettors favor, and which teams are in their disfavor.

The analysis is more complicated in professional sports than college due to the larger role of situational analysis. However, given time, public biases can usually be traced. So long as the constant feedback from bettors is incorporated in the linemaking process, the opening numbers won't be too far off.

Sometimes, linemakers react slowly to trends. As a result, linemakers are mistakenly cited for poor vision. Rather, the situation merely confirms that feedback plays a large role in the linemaking process. Bettors fail to play on recent events consistently, and linemakers respond accordingly. Were bettors to react more quickly, the opening numbers would reflect recent trends more strongly.

Today's computer databases have radically changed the ability of oddsmakers to be able to understand trend analysis. Formerly, records were kept in loose-leaf notebooks and checking a simple trend about how a team performed after playing a fifth game in seven nights would have been a tedious affair consuming many hours. Now, computer programs retrieve the needed data in seconds.

Creating odds is a balance between art and science. Computerized programs help develop power ratings for all sports teams. Yet, subjective analysis is still a large part of the linemaking process, due to the volatility in the sports handicapping field.

2

HOW THE LINES
ARE MOVED

by Vincent Magliulo
Former Sportsbook Director, Caesars Palace Las Vegas

In order to understand why line movement occurs in bookmaking, it is necessary to be aware of some important associated factors. It must first be pointed out that, although related, linemaking and bookmaking are two different aspects of a betting line.

Every line has two components: the proposition and the odds. The proposition is the actual event being booked, such as a ball game, boxing match, or a player to scoring the first touchdown in the Super Bowl. The odds portion of the line is the actual price of the event such as the point spread, money line or, in some cases, both.

In formulating the line, an oddsmaker will take into account talent, location (i.e. home field or court, neutral site), record, injuries, and the public's interest and perception of the event. There are also countless situations that come into play during the course of the year that have to be considered. One example is that bettors will likely bet on an NBA team that was beaten by 30 points or more in their previous game.

The purpose of the betting line is to balance the action. It is not a prediction of an event's outcome. Wagering is an opinion of bettors that is backed up with monetary gain in mind. As a bookmaker, the goal is to attract equal amounts of money on each side, not necessarily to split the opinions equally. In bookmaking, as in all casino games, there is a need to limit liability.

This is where line movement comes into play. It is rare that the opening line or price will attract equal amounts of money on both (or all) sides. Event limits in conjunction with line movement are used to limit liability.

In general, limit extensions will be the main factor in line movement. Bear in mind that the bigger the event, the higher the limit. This is why the Super Bowl will likely have less line movement than an NBA total, for example.

In football and basketball, the sports that attract the most wagering dollars, bettors put up $11 to win $10. Winning wagers collect $21. The following example will illustrate how line movement will occur when limit extensions are met. ($5,500 will constitute a limit play.) This example could illustrate wagering activity on a football or basketball game.

Matchup	Pointspread	Monies Wagered	New Pt Spread
LA		-0-	
NY	-4	$5,500 to win $5,000	-4 1/2
LA		$550 to win $500	
NY	-4 1/2	$5,500 to win $5,000	-5
LA		$5,500 to win $5,000	
NY	-5	-0-	-4 1/2
LA		$2,750 to win $2,500	Game Time
NY	-4 1/2	$2,200 to win $2,000	Wagering Ends

The opening line in this example shows New York as a 4-point favorite. The opening line was moved from four to four and a half when a limit play was made on New York. The betting continued to be predominant on New York and the line went from four and a half to 5. At 5, Los Angeles money shows and the line goes back to four and a half where money is wagered on both teams.

When wagering ends at post time, there is a total of $8,800 bet on Los Angeles and $13,200 bet on New York. If Los Angeles covers, the house wins $5,200. Should New York cover, the house stands to lose $3,200.

Throughout the wagering on this event, the bookmaker must also pay attention to who is wagering. Some bettors are more sophisticated than others and their opinions deserve more notice.

Again, the goal is to balance the action. It did not happen in this example, but the house exposure was limited by moving the line. Injuries to key players can also impact a wagering line. If an injury is known in advance, it will be incorporated in the opening line. For instance, if a team's starting point guard sustains an injury that will keep him out of the next game, it will likely translate into a 3-point swing in the opening betting line. If there is such an injury, it is obviously more advantageous to be aware of it in advance.

However, when such an injury occurs or becomes known after the wagering line has been posted and played into, it can prove to be costly to the house.

An example of this situation can be illustrated by using the same chart as above. New York opened as a 4-point favorite. When they were wagered upon to become a 5-point favorite, it was learned that Los Angeles' starting point guard would miss the game due to the flu. At this time the bookmaker will likely adjust the line as much as three points, making New York an eight point favorite and lowering the limit on the game.

Another situation that can cause line movement often occurs on the eve of league playoffs. When teams are jockeying for playoff position and games are being played the same day, but at different times, the results of the earlier games can greatly impact the wagering lines on the later games.

Therefore, it may be necessary to suspend wagering on afternoon games while morning games are being played. At the conclusion of the morning games, the results are evaluated and adjustments on the afternoon games' wagering lines may be necessary.

It is extremely important in Nevada's sports wagering environment for oddsmakers and bookmakers to work closely together to help maximize profitability and customer satisfaction. Clear lines of communication between oddsmakers and bookmakers will ensure that these goals are met.

3

THE REAL STORY BEHIND THE LINE

by Lem Banker
Professional Sports Bettor

When I first came to Las Vegas in 1957, there were only five legal sportsbooks in town, but plenty of "outlaw" bookmakers. You could bet as much as you wanted to lose. If the action was too high, the bookies would hedge some of the bets to other bookmakers throughout the country. At that time, interstate betting wasn't a federal offense. None of the hotels in Nevada wanted race or Sportsbooks in their successful casinos because they were afraid of possible interference from the feds—a fear that eventually happened.

In 1960, the federal government initiated a law against organized crime known as the "Kennedy Law," which made it a crime to place a bet from one state to another. They also imposed a 10 percent federal excise tax on all wagers. In addition, all bookmakers, whether legal or illegal, had to buy a $50 stamp each year to make it legal to book a bet. The stamp was actually one of the main reasons illegal bookies came out of the cellar.

That was a long time ago, and times have changed. Today, there are more than 100 legal sportsbooks in the state of Nevada. All big-time professional sports—baseball, football, and basketball—have increased their schedules. New franchises have been added. Seven-figure salaries, pension plans, commercial endorsements and astronomical television and radio contracts have made professional sports one of the biggest businesses in the world. With all of the new fans either attending the games, watching them on TV, or listening on their radios, there are more bookmakers. There are also new ways to bet: parlays, round robins, teasers, parlay cards, future bets and Super Bowl contests. Sports betting has grown into a huge business.

The biggest mystery throughout the betting world is how the official line is made. Many phonies try to take the credit. I've been asked how the line is made for over 50 years. The first bookmaker to deal a point spread line was Lou Hecht from Minneapolis in the late 1940's. It really caught on. Prior to that, the bookies would only put up a money line on close betting match-ups. The Green Sheet from Minneapolis was the first publication to print the power ratings and past performances of all college and professional teams. My good friend Mort Olshan was one of their handicappers and writers.

Years ago, most of the big betting offices around the country had three or more price makers on their payroll. Each handicapper was from a different part of the country, so they could read the regional newspapers and be informed of the teams in their areas. Also, the bookies didn't want the handicappers to be friendly with each other, because they were afraid of a possible conspiracy—that is, sending out bad prices and having their friends or agents beating the bookie with the phony numbers.

If one handicapper made a game minus four points, and the other odds maker came up with minus six points, the bookie would open the game minus five points in the middle. Then they would present the line to a handful of respected bettors early to get their reactions. If the players passed on any particular game, they felt the number was right. If the number was too high or too low, it would be flattened out before it reached the public.

For years and years, every so-called handicapper or odds maker I have known would rely on *The Gold Sheet*'s power ratings for their key source of information. Some of the handicappers may have known teams from their own section of the country, but they were ignorant regarding the numerous teams from other areas and conferences throughout the nation.

One day, a strange thing happened. The printer for *The Gold Sheet* made an honest typographical error. The University of Washington was playing UCLA in football. The printer gave Washington a minus 19 rating, instead of a minus 9. The lower the rating, the stronger the team. The early Las Vegas outlaw line came out 10 points off the right price. The bookmakers didn't know the difference. Ninety percent of the bookmakers around the country wouldn't know the right favorite from the wrong favorite.

The bookies got burned. Only after lopsided betting did they realize they had a bad price. But don't feel sorry for the bookies—they overcome everything. I've never heard of a bookmaker going broke though I have heard of plenty of players going busted. This printing error proved one thing—the so-called handicappers, without the help of *The Gold Sheet*, would be useless early in the season if it weren't for the yearlong research of the hundreds of teams that are dealt in the betting parlors throughout the state.

The bookies of Nevada have depended upon *The Gold Sheet* to guide them for almost five decades. Since sports betting has become one of the biggest attractions and businesses in the state of Nevada, I think that the late Mort Olshan, founder of *The Gold Sheet*, should be honored posthumously by one of our great universities. Forty-seven years of honesty and integrity that the bookmakers depend on shouldn't be forgotten.

4

SHOPPING SPORTSBOOKS FOR VALUE

You must be honest with yourself. If you're best isn't good enough, then you've got to find something else to do— another sport where you're best will be good enough.

-- Joe Namath

Talent is what you possess; genius is what possesses you.

--Malcolm Cowley

Value is a word you often hear in conversations around Las Vegas. In gambling, as in shopping, value is the objective we should always be striving for. I think the best way to describe value is ultimately getting the very best part of the available action.

Sportsbooks these days are bigger and better than ever. The focus within the casino industry is to catch the interest of sports bettors and to thrill them with wagers they cannot get anywhere else. Because we live in a country known for economic competition, and because Las Vegas is the world's capital for gambling, we gamblers can take advantage of the market availability of different wagers. For example, if you like the Dallas Cowboys and go into a sportsbook and find them at +6 points against the Cleveland Browns, why not shop around for +6 1/2 or +7 points?

You'd be surprised how much of a difference a half-point here and there can mean over the course of a season. It can make a loser into a winner—and vice-versa. When you make future wagers, always shop around to a minimum of three sportsbooks for the best odds. It's amazing how many future odds and propositions can vary from casino to casino. Many casinos offer different situations that can be used to your advantage. If you play parlay cards (which I don't recommend), ties win in some books, but lose in others. Read the card carefully before playing it!

It is usually better to wager early on favorites and wait until later to bet underdogs. Favorite players tend to be a part of the herd mentality, and rush to the windows just before the game.

Every book in town offers lines on games. Some have a 10-cent line, others a 15-cent line. Since these lines vary, the smart gambler will always shop around to find the best value for his gaming dollar.

Sportsbooks also offer interesting wagers to promote activity in their casinos. A few of these exotic betting opportunities offered by the Rio, Caesars Palace, the Riviera and the Aladdin are detailed here to serve as examples of what you might expect to find on one of your visits to the books of Vegas. Of course, just because the wager appears to be interesting, you must always delve deeper into the proposition to discover whether it offers you good value.

The Rio one season offered a 50-1 shot on a no-hitter being pitched on a given day. If any team got no hits, you won. Another interesting wager was the heavy hitters contest offered at Caesars Palace, which featured two teams who were going to be playing a weekend series. The two heavy hitters, one from each team, were pitted against each other.

For example, if the Mets were playing the Cubs on Friday, Saturday and Sunday, Caesars put the line out on the Mets best hitter vs. the Cubs counterpart. The player would get one point for each home run and one point for each RBI—the most points win. Obviously, pitching match-ups were a very important part of your handicapping. This game-within-a-game was fun and worth a look.

YOU CAN BET ON IT!

The Riviera offered a different proposition every day, although I can't comprehend how they came up with all those exotic wagers. One of them was total combined hits of the top three sluggers when the Pirates and Giants played. The over-under on this bet was three and a half hits with over at -125 and under at +105.

Of course, all three players had to start or no action. I found these bets to be "mind candy"—very tasty to think about, as long as you didn't become too accustomed to the taste of sweets. In other words, check them out and take a shot once in a while, but beware of the 20-cent line because it's too much to give up in most cases.

At the Aladdin's Friday-Saturday-Sunday contest you had to pick a team consisting of three outfielders, four infielders, one catcher and a player from a miscellaneous position or designated hitter. Your team could earn points as follows: stolen base, one point; single, one point; double, two points; triple, 3; home run, 4; with a bonus of five points for a grand slam.

There is a lot of illusion in the casino, and all that glitters is not gold. Shop around to find the best deal for your dollar. Or, as Lem Banker, one of the greatest shoppers for value in the history of sports betting, advises, "What you save is what you earn." Consider this a message written in stone. Always get the best value for your hard earned money!

5

REALISTIC GOALS AGAINST THE LINES

by Steve Fezzik
Professional Handicapper & Bettor

I see it in virtually every tout's website. They win, and they win big. The bad apples discuss how they are "documented" with a winning percentage at or above 70 percent. The better apples discuss how they expect to hit more realistic winning rates of 56-60 percent.

The same occurs for individual bettors. When asked, bettors often respond that they expect to hit around 60 percent of their plays. I give all these guys an A for optimism. Unfortunately, they are delusional in their expectations.

Setting a goal for a realistic winning percentage is a tricky thing, since theoretically winning percentages should be able to rise well above 60 percent. If someone has the competency and the know-how, why shouldn't they be able to win consistently at 62 percent? The best evidence I can offer is based on real world observations.

The most successful publicly known betting syndicate was "the computer group." These guys made millions and millions betting into soft numbers with a state of the art computer program.

They hit 57-59 percent, and raked in the cash along the way. Since then, the point spreads have gotten considerably sharper across the board. "Everyone" is using computer models, and lines that are off by 2.5 or more points are becoming very, very rare.

YOU CAN BET ON IT!

Heck, there are even places out there making money dealing sports with minus 105 vigorish! These lines are getting sharper each year. If one of the best betting syndicates in the world, playing against softer lines in the past, was "only" able to win at 58 percent, it is not a stretch to see that a realistic top winning percentage for everyone else is well below this level. Do you know what a bettor could make hitting at 60 percent? Let's assume you start with $1,000 you were planning to buy a couch with. Instead, you decide to take a pot shot with it.

You choose to play only one game a day, and wager what would normally be an insane 10 percent of bankroll on each play, laying -110. A little over five years later you wind up with a 1200-800 record (60 percent ATS). Guess how much money your $1,000 will grow to? $10,000? $50,000? Nope. $550 billion. Yes, that's BILLION. It sounds ridiculous, but believe me the math completely supports it.

Now the above analysis doesn't prove that it cannot be done, however, it surely must put the burden of proof onto those claiming they hit 60 percent of their plays. Given the above, how could they not have accumulated a large fortune? You hear the same tired excuses over and over.

- *They can hit 60 percent, but are too streaky, and the few bad runs wipe them out.* Sorry, I'm not buying it. In the above example, all you need is a 1200-800 record. Any order of wins and losses will produce the same final results.

- *They have poor money management.* Sorry, again I simply don't accept it. As my numbers show, having an ability to hit at 60 percent is akin to owning a printing press full of money. Even with some lousy money management, you should still make a small fortune (instead of a large fortune).

- *No one could bet millions on one game without the line moving.* It's a good argument, and I concur. However, this only becomes a problem after one has clearly sailed into easy street multimillionaire status.

So the next time a guy tells you he is a 60 percent handicapper, you might want to confirm whether he is a multimillionaire. If he isn't, it is likely he either: 1) Cannot hit 60 percent or 2) is one horrific money manager.

What's interesting is that several people offer up "proof" of 60 percent plus handicappers by pointing at one-year performances in monitored contests and picks as "proof" that this competency level has been attained. What they miss is that during any small sample size like this, routine variance will result in many contestants hitting 60 percent.

Some will be good handicappers, some even not so good. However, all will regress to the mean going forward in future years. Flip a coin 100 times, and you will get 64 heads, provided you flip enough coins along the way.

60 percent is simply not obtainable on any large volume of bets vs. widely available lines. In fact, I personally feel that the better handicappers and bettors are only able to achieve a long-term win rate that is around 55 percent against market lines. It sounds depressing, but I've got good news.

With even a 53 percent win rate, you can make a lot of money on your bets provided you utilize reduced vigorish, rogue lines, free half point promotions, and other betting methods.

As a closing statement, I would love to be proven wrong here, and have any handicapper or bettor step to the plate and show how he is able to hit 58-60 percent of his plays going forward over an extended period of time with a large volume of plays. I'm rooting for it to happen. I'm already planning my trip to the airport to pick out my personal Learjet!

YOU CAN BET ON IT!

I should add a quick caveat to this entire article. There are select unique 60 percent plus type plays that do occur out there. However, these are very few and far between, and typically do not occur.

Rather, they tend to be things like arena football bets, golf proposition bets, individual player proposition bets, etc. My focus is addressing the top winning percentages achievable when betting sides and totals vs. the major sports out there— markets that have a great deal of liquidity where bettors can place large bets down without huge line movements.

6

WINNING $100,000

by Bill Brown
Computer Expert & Author

A caller to a local sports-talk radio shows asked "How much would I have to bet to win $100,000 a year?"

There are three major variables involved in this calculation: 1) expected winning percentage; 2) the amount of your betting unit; and 3) how many bets per week-month-year you make. Since the result varies as you vary any of the three, it may be simpler to "back into" a third variable by using two known values and then calculating the third. For example, we'll pick a winning percentage of 60 percent—a percentage very few will ever reach, but a little on the high side to affirm how tough it is to make a living betting sports even at an excellent winning percentage—and decide on our betting unit, which we'll say is $550.

Using the table on the next page, we see that after 100 bets, we will be ahead $8,000 (table calculations take into consideration the 11-10 lay). Dividing our goal of $100,000 by our $8,000 win gives us a factor of 12.5, meaning we'll have to make 1250 bets (roughly 25 bets a week) using our 60 percent, $550 to reach our $100,000 profit goal.

You can calculate how much you'll win a week-month-year by taking the amount you win per 100 bets and adjusting it to your number of bets during that period. For example, if you make 400 bets during football season, wager $220 a bet and past history shows you pick 58 percent winners, you should win $9,440 for the season ($2,360 per 100 bets, times four).

YOU CAN BET ON IT!

For larger wagers, multiply the amount won by the factor of your bet. Example, a $3,300 player (use the $330 column) winning 59 percent will win $41,700 per 100 bets.

Since not all bettors are flat bettors, this table may not be of help to them. It will, however, give those who play football and basketball an indication of how tough it is to make a living as a professional gambler.

100 Bets of the Following Amounts

BET AMOUNT

%	$110	$220	$330	$440	$550
55	550	1100	1650	2200	2750
56	760	1520	2280	3040	3800
57	970	1940	2910	3880	4850
58	1180	2360	3540	4720	5900
59	1390	2780	4170	5560	6950
60	1600	3200	4800	6400	8000
61	1810	3620	5430	7240	9050
62	2020	4040	6060	8080	10100
63	2230	4460	6690	8920	11150
64	2440	4880	7320	9760	12200
65	2650	5300	7950	10600	13250
66	2860	5720	8580	11440	14300
67	3070	6140	9210	12280	15350
68	3280	6560	9840	13120	16400
69	3490	6980	10470	13960	17450
70	3700	7400	11100	14800	18500

CHAPTER

2

MAKING MONEY: GENERAL WINNING CONCEPTS

1

30 RULES FOR SUCCESS

by Sonny Reizner

Past Director, Race and Sports Castaways,
Rio Desert Inn Hotels Las Vegas

All vices are of personal origin. Playing cards do not make the gambler, nor a bottle of liquor the drunkard.

-- Anonymous

Anything good is developed slowly.

-- Sebastian Coe

Egotism is the anesthetic that deadens the pain of stupidity.

-- Knute Rockne

It always amazes me that the same person who will examine, touch, and ask numerous questions when considering making a purchase and then says, "I might be back; I'm going to look around further," will go to a sportsbook, take a quick look at the board, think for just a moment about the odds, and then plunk down a sizable amount of money on the outcome of a game. Even though a wrong choice results in a total loss, the expertise involved and the time and effort expended in making that choice is minimal.

Over a period of time, it is almost impossible for the unknowledgeable player to win. It's not easy for even the informed, hard-working and dedicated sports bettor. The following rules of sports betting developed and tested through many years of experience, will not ensure winning. But observing these rules and adhering to the disciplines described will help any sports bettor enormously. In almost every undertaking, there is a correct way and an incorrect way. Naturally, the correct way offers a better chance to succeed. If you find these rules too difficult to understand or abide by, then my most conscientious and wholehearted advice is to play for minimal amounts, have fun and be happy.

On the following pages are my 30 Rules for Success in Sports Betting.

1. Understand what must be overcome

The bettor must not only know that the 11-10 proposition gives him a negative expectancy of about four and a half percent, but he must also learn to understand, through experience, what that means. The bookmaker's edge is not unassailable, but neither is it negligible. It need not be feared, but cannot be taken lightly.

2. Knowledge of the game

The game itself, not only the scores and the results, must be studied in all its complexities.

3. Remember your goals

Personal goals should influence the way you play. A different approach is required in playing for a living, compared with trying to make a "quick score." Betting for fun is different than betting for profit.

4. Dedication

To be a long-term successful sports bettor, one must be completely dedicated. There is no way to circumvent the considerable hard work involved. The romance and lure of "easy money" should be recognized as a delusion. If you think it's easy, you certainly don't know enough about it.

5. Stay informed

Subscribe to and read all the pertinent publications about the sports you bet. This might involve reading as many as 20 different newspapers and periodicals on a regular basis.

6. Pay attention

Watch or listen to as many games as possible, in an objective manner. They all contribute to your over-all knowledge.

7. Money management

The most important part of sports betting is money management. Almost every successful money management method will require that you bet more when you're winning and that you back off when you're losing. Doubling up to catch up is the worst approach. Don't be afraid to take a loser or a losing day.

8. Be aware of cycles

Accept the fact that good and bad results are part of the game, and that winning and losing streaks happen in cycles.

9. Have a good attitude

Have confidence in your own opinion, but give weight to the judgment of others before and after you form your own opinion.

10. Stay in shape

Keep your body toned mentally and physically. It is as important for the bettor to be in condition as it is for the athlete.

11. Don't try to get even on any one game

You should tend to bet less after losing. Sonny says, "Winners beget winners and losers beget losers."

12. Learn how to get value

Serious sports betting is not a leisure-time activity. You cannot always do what is convenient. You must learn where and when and how to bet games at the most favorable situation. This takes a great deal of time and effort.

13. Be inquisitive

Ask questions. Learn why a line moves one way or another.

14. Be knowledgeable

Don't bet in the dark. For example, check lineups, health of players and ability of replacements.

15. Have discipline

It is almost impossible to win if you bet every game on TV or radio. If you must bet all TV games, I suggest you form a distinct category of bet for those contests—I call them "pleasure bets." Bet only 10 percent of your normal wager if you have no good reason to make a bet other than that the game can be seen on TV.

16. Avoid sentimental bets

These are even worse than pleasure bets. If your alma mater means so much to you, you should get enough fun out of just rooting.

17. Understand mathematics and percentages

You should understand the value of points and half-points and, specifically, the points and half-points when tacked on or subtracted from specific numbers. A half-point subtracted from or added to three or four in football is much more significant than the same half-point applied to an eight or 9.

18. Vary bets in different amounts

Extra factors make certain plays worth larger bets than others.

19. Look for psychological factors.

Momentum, injuries, weather, dissension, travel hardship, contract disputes—all these things can alter normal performance expectations.

20. Outside problems

If you are undergoing serious personal problems such as poor health, marital difficulties, undue financial worries, etc., don't bet.

21. Avoid distractions

Always be aware of and try to avoid outside distractions. Anything that affects your concentration is a hazard to successful sports wagering.

22. Watch sporting events objectively

Even though your money is on one side, try to see the games without prejudice. It will help you next time. There will be games you will lose when you should have won, and games you will win when you should have lost.

23. There is no law of averages

Every sporting event is its own distinct and separate entity. There is no such thing as "due to win" or "due to lose." A team will win when it gets things together, not because it lost five in a row.

24. Watch for trends and streaks

Try to discover and take advantage of trends before they are written and talked about. To take advantage of a trend, you must be among the first to recognize it.

25. Do not accept rumor for fact

Many sports stories are just that—only stories. You must make every effort to find out if a rumor is true before you invest money on its strength.

26. Maintain a home court advantage

Do your handicapping and betting in comfortable surroundings. To do either in an environment in which you are not comfortable is like playing all your games on the road. Don't give away the home court advantage.

27. Stay collected

Don't panic when losing, and don't get cocky when winning. Remember, there's just an eyelash difference between one result and the other. Keeping a proper equilibrium will ultimately bring better results.

28. Be patient

Play to be there tomorrow. They play the Star Spangled Banner almost every day, but if you're tapped out, there is no tomorrow. Don't play as though there is no tomorrow, but also don't play as though you're going to live forever. A happy medium is best. And remember the old adage of sports betting: "If you bet slow, you're bound to go. If you bet fast, you won't last." Play to limit losses, not to limit winnings.

29. There is no such thing as a lock game

If a linemaker puts up a two-sided proposition, it should be apparent that either side might win.

30. Stay loose!

And one final word: If you're betting amounts that will change your personality or your standard of living, cut down. You're betting too much.

2

THE ABC'S OF
SPORTS HANDICAPPING

by Andrew Iskoe
Owner, *Logical Approach*

Welcome to my world.

Mine is a world of daily intrigue with many hours of hard work, but with immediate feedback, consisting of instant gratification or regrets. I am part mathematician, part psychologist. I try to forecast the behavior of not one, not two, not a few, but a rather large group of humans. I am a sports handicapper, and my daily task is to pick the winners of the many professional and college sporting contests held on an almost daily basis.

My job is not unique, although the amount of time I spend in researching and analyzing games separates me from a population that numbers literally in the millions who follow sports. Many follow a favorite team or teams and are truly fans of the sport.

Quite a growing number of enthusiasts are involved in "fantasy" leagues, assembling teams that compete mythically in accumulating statistics based on individual players. Finally, there is a growing group of sports enthusiasts who back their opinions with money.

Wagering on sports is legal in the state of Nevada, and Las Vegas is the sports wagering capital. Over the years, many people have tried to come to Vegas and break the bank, but it just doesn't happen that way. The vast majority of those who wager (some estimates are as high as 90 percent) lose on a regular basis. Only a small percentage are able to turn a profit, and an even smaller percentage, perhaps two to three percent at the very most, are able to earn a living from wagering on sports.

Reality is not quite as bleak as the picture of gloom and doom that I've painted. There are many reasons why those who try fail, and lessons that can be learned to give you a better chance to win on your next trip out west. Perhaps the best way of expressing some of the key concepts involved in becoming one of the winners is to get back to basics. Let's review the ABC's of sports handicapping.

A Is for Attitude

You must have both a positive and a realistic attitude. It's easy to get discouraged when you become aware of just what the realities of sports wagering are. A success rate of 58-60 percent is quite good, but it means you're still unsuccessful about 40 percent of the time. It's easy to get discouraged when you hit those inevitable losing streaks, yet it is exactly at this time that you must be positive and show confidence in your proven abilities. Don't be over-confident, but don't be easily discouraged.

B Is for Basics

If you are going to be successful in sports handicapping, you need to be well versed in the basics of both the sports you will be handicapping and the world of sports wagering. You can't just jump in and become an instant expert. You need to do the background work, assemble the historic data and become as familiar as possible with the sports you'll be tracking. This means that you must understand how the sport is played, the strategies involved, the personalities involved, and so on.

As to the handicapping basics, you must be thoroughly familiar with the basic concepts, such as vigorish, parlay, teaser, round robin, pushes, buying a half point, etc. Before you can ever hope to become a master of the trade, you must commit the basics to memory.

C Is for Creativity

While handicapping may seem to be a cut and dried exercise of mathematical analysis and comparisons, the truth is that the very best handicappers all have a creative streak inside of them that is constantly causing them to look at things in a new light.

In many ways, handicapping is like science, whereby you come up with a thought, formulate ideas about what it means, research the past, and draw conclusions. Creativity is the one singular concept that will ultimately enable you to rise above the vast majority of handicappers, because you will uncover some powerful relationships that point to success.

D Is for Discipline

One of the most important fundamentals you will ever learn is discipline. Although this might seem to contradict the concept of creativity, it actually serves as a reinforcement. Discipline is the ability to develop a style of handicapping and making selections, and not deviating from the criterion you establish. That doesn't mean steadfast entrenchment in a particular style.

Rather, it means that you should not force a selection because "it looks good." It means not making a play on a game simply because it's on TV. It means sitting out a weekend of football if there are no solid plays according to your method of handicapping. It's not making a play on the Super Bowl just because it's the Super Bowl, if you don't have an edge.

It also means sticking to your own opinions and not being unduly influenced by others. Believe me, in the long run, this ability will keep you off many, many more losers than the winners your restraint may cause you to miss.

E Is for Experience

The one thing you can't gain from a book, seminar or discussion with fellow handicappers is experience. Only time can give you the necessary experience from which you will subconsciously build a mental library of events that are similar to, or different from, upcoming events that will enable you to draw upon those experiences and events from the past. Sure, it takes time. But in every line of work, you must pay your dues, and being patient will have its rewards down the road.

F Is for Focus

In order to attain consistency in your handicapping, you must remain focused on your objectives. In a sense, it is similar to the concept of discipline in that you must be able to filter out distractions that may arise. Develop focus by writing your goals on paper, whether they are long or short term, and the methods by which you seek to attain them. Don't get discouraged by any pitfalls you may encounter along the way.

G Is for Goals

You must clearly define your goals. Are you looking for a main source of income, or are you looking to just supplement your current income? Or are you handicapping just for fun?

If you don't know where you are going, how can you possibly know when you get there? By clearly defining your goals, you will be better able to chart your progress along the way, knowing when to make adjustments. At the same time, you'll be developing discipline.

H Is for Handicapping

A structured approach or format is essential to the process of picking the most likely winner of a sporting contest. There are several types of handicapping approaches—statistical, fundamental, and trends are just a few. Most good handicappers use a combination of these approaches, with one of them forming the foundation.

But in order to be successful, you must be aware that there are always good reasons for playing the side that is opposite the one you've selected. Be objective and realize that there is no such thing as a "lock" or a "can't miss" game. A good way of doing this is to list the reasons for a play on a sheet of paper. After you've completed this task, if you find there are no reasons to play one of the sides, pass that game.

Unintentionally, you are being biased. There are always good reasons to play each side. As a good handicapper, your job is to evaluate those reasons and make a decision based on which of those factors is most likely to come into play in a particular game.

J Is for Journal

Keep a journal, or diary, to record your growth as a handicapper. Record your mistakes as well as your successes. After a game, write your thoughts on why you were right or wrong. It's silly to think that months, or even weeks, after an event, we can remember details of a particular game that pointed something out to us.

One way of keeping a journal is to use a microcassette recorder into which you can verbalize your thoughts. "This is what I liked about this team, but I failed to look at this." Or, "I didn't give enough weight to this factor." Or, "I forgot that this key player was still going to be out." And so forth.

The best way to avoid repeating mistakes is to be aware of them. A journal helps you to remember. The best way to build upon a concept that may have promise is to recall what thoughts you had when you came up with that brilliant idea. A journal allows you to capture your thoughts for future reference.

No two games are identical, but many are surprisingly similar. A journal helps you track and recall the mental processes of handicapping you will want to use again and again.

K Is for Knowledge

There is no substitute for knowledge. In many cases, it means keeping records of performance, which can be a painstaking process that consumes hours each day, depending on the sport. But this process is part of the key to developing the experience you'll need to refer back to when similar situations arise in the future. Read newspapers and annual periodicals. Get as much information as you can and sift through it to glean key bits of knowledge that you can use later.

L Is for Luck

As much as we don't want to admit it, a great part of being a successful handicapper involves having good luck, but only in the sense that roughly half of all games are decided by luck, regardless of how much effort you put into your handicapping. You just have to accept it.

What about the other half of the games? Those are the ones that will depend upon your handicapping. That is, if you can hit most of the games in which luck doesn't play a part in the outcome, you will have the kind of success it takes to show a profit. We handicap all games and look for them to go according to our handicapping. We must realize that about half of these games will, but the other half won't.

Good handicappers will zero in on those games most likely to go to form, but still realize that they may also be subject to random luck. Luck, good or bad, inevitably comes into play. That's why we can't be discouraged when we hit a slump, or get too ecstatic when we're on a roll. Luck can, and often does, change overnight. What we must do is strive for consistency in an effort to reduce the number of games decided by luck to a minimum.

M Is for Money Management

Another critical concept to master, money management is as important as making selections. Many a handicapper can pick winners, but fail to show profits because of poor money management. Many books have been written on money management, and you would do well to review several of the theories espoused by the authors. Find a method with which you feel comfortable, and then exercise the discipline to follow it. Good money management can increase your return by as much as 3-5 percent.

N Is for Niche

We can't all be experts in all things. We should find out what we do best, and then concentrate on being the best we can in that field. In handicapping, we find our niche by observing our strengths and weaknesses. Perhaps we are better handicappers in college football, or possibly the NBA. Or maybe we do well in college football, but excel in a couple of the major conferences such as the SEC and ACC. It would be to our best advantage to concentrate on just a few areas rather than try to cover all the bases. Find your niche. Become an expert. Maybe it will be a few teams in several sports. Perhaps you will concentrate on just one or two sports.

You will increase your proficiency as a handicapper by focusing on what you do best. As you gain experience, you can expand. For me, it was football, then basketball, then baseball. But it took over ten years for me to feel comfortable in all three sports. Remember, it's not how much you know, it's how successful you are. It takes time. Give it time.

O Is for Organization

To be successful in any line of work, you must be organized—this is essential. Organization is especially true in handicapping sports, which requires you to keep detailed records on many, many teams over the course of a season. As you develop as a handicapper, you will revise the information you keep and what you believe is important. But because so many of the sports are played on a daily basis or (with the exception of football) several times a week, you need to be up to speed.

You cannot afford to fall behind in your record keeping. As you will discover before too long, current form is an essential factor to consider when assessing an upcoming event. If your records are not up to date, you will not be able to correctly assess current form, regardless of the method you use.

The key to complete and efficient record keeping is organization, be it through notebooks, computers or a combination.

Regardless, you must be prepared before a season starts with a plan for gathering information and organizing it into a usable form. Most professionals spend a month or two getting ready for an upcoming season. Much like the athletes, we as handicappers also need our "spring training," during which we prepare for the rigors of the season ahead.

P Is for Probabilities

Probabilities form the foundation of what we do. In effect, we are mathematicians who determine what the probability is of a certain team covering the spread. Some of us do it structurally, by assigning a mathematical weight or formula to each game, and then selecting those that give us the greatest likelihood of being correct.

A great many of the top handicappers do it more intuitively, relying on experience and repeated occurrences of similar situations, and then assign a high or a low degree of probability to an event. Of course, we always keep in mind that it takes approximately 52.4 percent winners to overcome Old Man Vig.

Hopefully, our handicapping evolves to a point where we can consistently play on games that have a 60 percent probability factor or higher. That number is quite good and still involves battling the element of luck. But if we can get to a point where we have a probability of 60 percent in our favor, we'll do very well. It takes time to master the factors involved in developing a true probability. That's where creativity and research come into play.

Q Is for Quiet

This seems simple enough, but it is very important. You need to be able to think clearly and make well-founded decisions. Thus, you must work in a quiet environment, devoid of distractions. Perhaps you have an office in your home, or a room that can be used where you will not be disturbed.

It is important that you be able to fully concentrate on what you are doing, be it updating your records or analyzing your data as you prepare to make a selection on a game. You'll also find that working in a quiet environment will enable you to become more efficient, getting more done in a shorter period of time, and thereby freeing up additional time for other activities or for some creative thinking.

R Is for Research

Research is the backbone of all handicapping. In order to best predict what may happen in the future, it is essential to know what has happened in the past. In handicapping, we try to liken the current game situation to similar situations from the past. How did this team react in that setting? How have all teams in similar situations fared in the past?

You should have past performance information available to you for this purpose. Initially, you should purchase this information from an outside source such as the Gambler's Book Club in Las Vegas, which has many back years' worth of results.

As you handicap, you will keep your own records to build upon your foundation of knowledge. Along the way, you will develop techniques for retrieving that data when you need to find answers to questions.

While the personal computer is ideal for this task, many handicappers still use hand-written notebooks in which they keep records, trends, notes, etc., about specific teams and games so that they can be quickly recalled long after they have faded from conscious memory. This concept is closely related to organization in that, the better organized you are, the better the research you will be able to conduct. It's all inter-related.

S Is for Science

Handicapping is both an art and a science. The science of handicapping is in the development of Power Ratings or other analytical data that can be used in assessing the likely outcome of a game. The art is in the interpretation of the data. You can't have one without the other. Good handicappers may rely on either the art or the science to a greater degree, but all handicappers make use of both areas in their selection process.

Even the scientific part of handicapping is an art, as in being creative or ingenious in developing new methods for analysis or record keeping. The Art-Science relationship is similar to the concept of Left-Right Brain. Individually, the two sides of the brain can give you only a part of the picture or a piece of the puzzle. But when they are combined, they allow you to extract the maximum for your mental powers.

T Is for Technology

Specifically the computer. The personal computer is ideally suited for two industries: stock market forecasting and sports handicapping. Both rely on the accumulation of vast amounts of data and the ability to sort through that data to extract pertinent info about the subject matter.

I strongly advise anyone who is serious about being a sports handicapper to invest in a computer with database and spreadsheet programs. While some people are better suited to keeping records and journals with a pencil and paper, computers are by far the most efficient way of keeping track of the information you will need to review on a regular basis.

Don't be mystified by computers, for they are just machines that do what you tell them to do—but they do it much faster. In handicapping a weekend of 40 college and 14 pro games, it might take 20 hours to do by hand what the computer can do in a few minutes. Time is an important ally. Computers save time. Take advantage of modern technology—the linesmakers do.

U Is for Unbiased Opinions

When it comes to evaluating an upcoming game objectively, it is very hard to forget our biases. Perhaps we were on the wrong side the last time these teams played. Being unbiased means that you must realize that both teams have a chance of being on the right side in every game.

As handicappers, we must assess the reasons for selecting each side, and then determine which set of reasons is likely to be most valid or applicable. Most of us grew up as fans of particular teams. The transition from being a fan to being an unbiased observer is not always easy. But it is essential, if you are to become a successful handicapper.

Earlier, I mentioned the practice of writing down the reasons for playing each side in a game. After you've spent some time thinking about it, if you come up with no reasons for one of the teams, you'd probably do best to pass the game.

You are being subconsciously biased. When I handicap a game, I try to list all the reasons for playing each side and then make my selection, keeping in mind that I'll be going against some convincing reasons for the other side. That's where experience comes in.

Remember, if you took the 100 best handicappers in the nation and had them handicap the Super Bowl, for example, you'd probably end up with a 60-40 split. That means, even though the majority of experts sided with Team A, there was still a substantial number who disagreed. There are valid reasons for each side, but you must not allow biases to influence your decisions.

V Is for Vigorish

Old Man Vig is that 10 percent commission we must pay on all straight wagers. 11-10, as it's known, translates to a winning percentage of 52.38 percent, the amount needed to break even. At a winning percentage greater than 52.38 percent, we begin to profit.

But our true winning percentage for breaking even is more likely around 55 percent when we consider the costs associated with handicapping, such as our overhead, out of pocket expenses and time. A full-time handicapper puts in 70-80 hours per week (often more), and there is a cost, or wage, associated with that time.

For handicapping to be a truly profitable exercise, we must factor in these costs and accept the fact that while the vig is a fixed cost of doing business, one that must be paid regardless of other expenses, the true costs are higher, and we must overcome those additional costs by hitting a higher percentage of winners. That's why if we set a goal of 60 percent and use that as our target range, we can accept a true rate of 57-58 percent, which is more than enough to pay Old Man Vig, cover our costs, and show a slight profit.

W Is for Winning

After all, winning's the name of the game! It's what they pay off on—the bottom line. Of course, the best team doesn't always win and, regardless of how good a handicapper you become, there will be game after game that "just doesn't figure."

Accept those games and go on because, as I said earlier, luck plays a great part in determining the outcome of half of all games. It's what you do with the other half—those that do go essentially according to form—that will be the indicator of your success as a handicapper.

Remember that in the vast majority of games in the major sports, the winner also covers the spread. In the NFL, for example, the favorite wins and covers, or the underdog wins outright, over 80 percent of the time. In less than one of every five games does the favorite win but fail to cover.

Gear your research towards trying to determine which factors govern the winning of games. It's a bit different in baseball where you lay or take odds, but for the major sports involving pointspreads (basketball and football), look towards uncovering the factors that are best able to predict a winning performance.

You should use as guides the many trends, angles and situations that you find in your research. And work on constructing a "Winning Profile" for each team in each sport—what are their individual strengths and weaknesses? Look for the most favorable and unfavorable factors. It all leads back to the concepts of organization, discipline and money management.

Of all the concepts presented in this article, those three are essential building blocks for success. Work hard: be a winner!

X Is for Expectations

Okay, so we fudged a little because we're running low on letters and "xylophone" isn't appropriate. By expectations, we mean you should realize that athletes' performances and your own handicapping results are both cyclical.

There will be winning streaks and losing streaks, highs and lows. You'll win games for the wrong reasons and lose games for the right reasons. Sports are still unpredictable. Humans are not robots, and thus consistent performances according to potential are the exception rather than the rule.

If you can be successful 53 percent of the time, you will break even. At 55 percent, you will show a slight profit. At 58 percent, you are doing well and at 60 percent winners, you are doing outstandingly well. Don't be misled by claims of 70 percent, 80 percent or 90 percent winners. It just doesn't happen except over a very short period.

If you are able to consistently hit between 55 percent and 60 percent winners, you'll do very well. Those are realistic expectations and should be your goal. Don't get easily discouraged.

If you're on to something, you will inevitably endure setbacks, but don't give up on what might seem a promising concept. Expect that you will have cold spells, but also expect that your hard efforts will be rewarded. They will.

Y Is for Yourself

Know yourself. Be yourself. Express yourself. Your success depends upon you and your commitment. The harder you work, the luckier and better you'll become. Define your goals. Determine your strengths and weaknesses and learn from them. Find your niche. No one but you can control the you factor.

Like most occupations, being a successful handicapper requires hard work. Most professional handicappers put in 80-hour weeks! That's a lot of time.

Are you that dedicated? If so, the self-satisfaction you will get over the years is tremendous. There are few better feelings than knowing you are right most of the time. In handicapping, we are fortunate in that we get virtually immediate feedback on our efforts. We don't have to wait weeks, months or years to see the results of our efforts. Handicapping is a fascinating experience with many rewards. You are in control of what you evaluate and how you evaluate. The possibilities are endless. But it all depends on you!

Z Is for ZZZZZZ's

That's right, sleep. Don't overwork yourself. Be sure to get enough rest. Allow your head to clear. Try tackling that question in the morning. In fact, overall good health has a positive correlation to successful handicapping. By being able to think clearly, you will come to better conclusions and make better decisions. By taking time to rest and then look at the same material with a "different set of eyes," you'll very often see things that you might not otherwise catch. Rest is a very important, yet often overlooked, aspect of our job. So be sure to get some every night: you'll be a better handicapper for it.

Conclusion. Well, we've covered a lot of ground. Although it might seem like a lot to review, each of these 26 concepts could easily have merited a description the length of this entire piece. By reviewing these concepts regularly, by trying to master as many as you can, and by implementing them, you will become a better handicapper. But remember, it does take time.

There are those of us in Las Vegas who are successful at what we do, but we've had to pay our dues, learn at the feet of others, and find things on our own which are suited to our individual styles and tastes. But there is a common thread that runs through all of us: we are a fiercely competitive group. We are always trying to do better today than we did yesterday, to have a better season this year than last. And we all love what we do.

Join us! There's plenty of room for everyone. Until there's the one perfect method that picks 100 percent winners in all games, the challenge is still there. It's a marvelous challenge and one that I look forward to taking every day.

3

18 FREQUENT MISTAKES IN SPORTS WAGERING

by Chuck Sippl
Senior Editor, *The Gold Sheet*

During my many years as a sports analyst, I have talked with and observed thousands of sports fans who enjoy wagering on games. And I've seen them make a lot of mistakes.

People love to talk sports. And many love to match wits with the oddsmaker. Everybody has an opinion. When they win a wager, that opinion is validated.

But if you're going to do anything more than throw a few dollars into the weekly football pool or make a friendly wager on a ball game, you've got to play the percentages if you expect to win. In fact, many sports bettors don't play the percentages. Instead, they often go into them. Therefore, it is usually very difficult for them to win anything other than an occasional wager.

Many useful books have been written on sports wagering that cover such basic topics as how to use power ratings, when to take the favorite, how to spot a "live" underdog, the value of the home field, etc. But I thought I'd turn things around a little bit here, assume the reader has at least a passing knowledge of sports betting, and focus on the most common errors of sports bettors.

Following is a brief rundown of some of the most frequently committed handicapping and wagering mistakes in sports betting.

1. Betting more than you can afford

Never bet the rent money or the food money. Know the size of your sports wagering bankroll, and don't exceed it. If your losses are forcing a change in your life-style or affecting other parts of your life, back off.

2. Getting blown out early in the season

Determine the size of your bankroll and try to restrain your enthusiasm early in the year. Avoid the temptation of betting too many games or too much money on the early games. Save a good portion of your bankroll for later in the year when you know more about the teams and the games are better defined.

3. Impulse betting

It's tough enough to beat the oddsmaker even when you have a thorough knowledge of sports and know the strengths and weaknesses of each team. Betting on a game just because you've "got a good feeling" is not the way to increase your income.

It is very unlikely that a novice or part-time handicapper is going to walk up to the window at a Nevada sportsbook and knock 'em dead. Bookmakers generally love impulse bettors because they're wrong much more often than they're right.

4. Chasing your money

This is the worst money-management mistake of all! Think about it a little bit. It's unlikely that you're going to get even by betting more money on spur-of-the-moment lower-percentage plays, than you do on your well-researched, high-percentage plays.

You can't win 'em all, but you can lose 'em all. If you bet on sports, it is inevitable you will have some losing days. Develop the maturity to deal with them. Remember, bookmakers want you to chase your money. If you're going to bet regularly, discipline yourself to take only high-percentage plays.

5. Betting on too many games

This is usually a sure way to get blown out, especially for the novice. Only bet on games that have substantial edges. You must discipline yourself to play percentages. Nevada sportsbooks love customers who are "all over the board." They want you to bet lots of totals, parlays and teasers as well. The more games and the more combinations, the better for the house.

The person the bookmaker dreads the most is the disciplined handicapper who makes substantial wagers on a few carefully chosen games with lots of nice edges. If sportsbooks encourage the undisciplined amateur and fear the knowledgeable "sharpshooter," what kind of bettor do you think you should try to be?

6. Betting on games just because they're on TV

If you must bet on TV games, you should use a smaller, "recreational" amount that is less than your normal betting unit, perhaps one-third or one-quarter of your normal wager. You'll win a few TV games and lose a few. But you shouldn't get recreational TV play mixed up with your well-handicapped games that have many more edges.

7. "Unloading" on a single game

There is no such thing as a "lock" in sports betting. Anyone who thinks there are "sure things" either has a very short memory or has never seen a fumble on a kickoff return, or an interception in the end zone, or a missed extra point, or a blocked field-goal attempt that goes the other way for a touchdown, or a key player injured early in a game, or an obviously incorrect referee's call, or the three-point shot that banks in, or an error, a walk and a three-run homer.

It's okay to bet a little more on your best games, but rarely is any one game worth more than twice as much as any other game. Anyone who unloads on a game and loses that bet will have an extremely difficult time making the percentages work for him. Don't play into the bookmaker's hands.

8. Over-emphasizing psychology

Psychology is a factor in sports handicapping. But it is not the only factor. And it is the decisive factor much less frequently than most people think. A team is only as good as its talent and chemistry. Psychology works best in handicapping when a team "had the guns" to make it work. Usually, when one team is, for whatever reason, fired up for a big effort, so is its opponent.

9. Counting on the must-win scenario

As one knowledgeable sports bettor once told me, "Must-win can't win." Very often, teams in so-called "must-win" situations are too "tight," and thus have difficulty performing at their best.

Opponents with nothing on the line, on the other hand, can afford to be "loosey-goosey" and take a lot of chances. The 1993 Miami Dolphins needed just one win in their last five games to make the playoffs. They still do.

10. Over-emphasizing technical trends

Tech trends are interesting. They can add a historical perspective. They can isolate characteristics that reflect the nature of the sport. They can help to identify high-percentage plays. But tech trends can by no means win games. Players and coaches win games. Most people who rely heavily on technical trends to determine their sports wagers do so because they don't really know how good the opposing teams are. In sports betting, current reality is always more important than history.

11. Overreacting to injuries

Remember, Thurman Thomas's backup at Oklahoma State was Barry Sanders. Just because one guy is out doesn't mean the next guy can't play. Besides, most teams get fired up when a key player is out. Teams are generally more vulnerable the second or third game after losing a key player than the first game.

Injuries become a telling factor when a team's key player is out for an extended period, or when a team is hit with a cluster of injuries at one or two positions.

12. Overreacting to recent performances

It was a wise man that first said, "No team is as good as it looks when it wins big, or as bad as it looks when it loses big." The week after a team wins big, the pointspread goes up and its next opponent is generally well focused.

The week after a team gets blown out, the pointspread goes down and the beaten team tends to practice harder, while its opponent can be lulled into a false sense of confidence.

13. Relying on too much youth

Newcomers often have that look of greatness. But it takes youngsters a few times around the block in both college and professional football before they start leading their teams to big wins in big games. Young quarterbacks in football and young point guards in basketball, no matter how talented they are, generally have problems in their first few games on the road and in big games, particularly against tough opposition.

14. Relying on too much offense

Offense is flashy. Makes for good highlights on ESPN, but a coach's best friend is a good defense. Defense takes the ball away and sets up easy scores in football. It prevents easy shots in basketball. And it limits scoring opportunities in baseball.

If a team has a good defense, it's generally in the ball game. Remember, it's who a team beats that means the most, not how big it wins.

15. Going against too much power

It's hard to make money in sports wagering if you always try to go against the best. The good teams tend to turn on the power in the big games. It's unwise to bet against the best teams too often.

You must choose your moments. It's hard to make a living by merely going with underdogs. A mix of motivated favorites and capable underdogs is usually the best recipe.

16. Forgetting which is the better team

A bettor can sometimes identify a lot of edges in a ball game. Revenge in a big rivalry is obvious. A great running back, a smart quarterback, an innovative coach or a great shooter or passer in basketball are all edges. But in most contests, the biggest edge of all is being the better team.

The bigger, faster, deeper teams win most games. They don't win them all, but they win a lot. Sports bettors should never fail to note which is the superior team in any contest. When the better team is the underdog, or is fired up against an inferior foe, you better think twice before going against it.

17. Underestimating the home field advantage

The value of the home fans and the home field is generally the greatest when the host team is either a small favorite or a small underdog; when the fans and the players know victory is possible, but will be difficult to achieve. It is often in those types of games that the hometown players feed off the energy of the crowd and benefit most from big plays and any swings in momentum.

18. Betting on bad numbers

The people in Las Vegas who bet on sports for a living know it's virtually impossible to win with "bad numbers." If you like the favorite in a game, and the pointspread is inflated, perhaps it's best to reduce your wager or avoid the game entirely. If you like the underdog in a game, and the pointspread is substantially reduced, maybe you should re-examine your wager or look for another game. It's good to have more than one outlet.

Learn how to use power ratings so you can determine whether you're getting value in the line or giving up value. Learn to anticipate the "public." If you like a side of a game the public likes, try to bet early and avoid the anticipated move in the pointspread.

If the side you like is not the "public" side, play late and try to get some additional value. Last, if you're going to bet a lot of money on a lot of games just about every day, you should consider moving to Las Vegas where you can shop, shop, shop for the best numbers, just as the pros do.

There you have it. If you pay attention to this checklist and take it to heart, your chances of profiting in your battle against the oddsmaker should be substantially increased.

4

HANDICAPPING SUCCESS FORMULA

by Mike Lee

Publisher & Chief Handicapper, *The Moneymaker*

The only way I know how to keep football fun is to win.
That's the only answer. There is no laughter in losing.
-- Darrell Royal

I want to win. That's it, all of it.
-- Al Davis

If you use a combination of mathematics plus intangibles in your selection process, you stand an excellent shot at achieving an elusive 60 percent mark against the spread—a number that will bring profits to your game.

Let's take a look at what you should use in your mathematical approach to achieve these results.

Power Ratings

For many years, I have used power ratings in my quest for the 60 percent barrier. The first place to begin when analyzing a game is with numbers. It is critical for a handicapper to have a firm mathematical base on which to formulate an opinion. Power ratings provide such a base.

Many sports publications provide readers with a weekly power rating section. These ratings are updated weekly based on various factors such as points for-against, injuries and win-loss records.

I try to take these ratings one step further by providing home-away power ratings on each team, especially in pro football, pro basketball and college basketball. Many teams play much differently on the road than at home. Some clubs are what I call "homers." These teams play much better at home than away. On the other hand, some teams play better on the road than in front of their home fans!

A number of lower echelon teams fall into this category, finding it easier to play on the road than in front of their own hostile home crowd. Bad teams rarely possess good home power ratings.

The best way to form your own power ratings is by using what I call the "margin" technique. The difference between points scored and points against is the margin. If a team wins by a 20-10 count of a 90 rated team, we have a +10 margin added to the 90 for a 100 rating.

If a team loses by 7-34 to a team with a 100-power rating, we deduct the margin of loss (27) from the 100 for a 73 rating. Again I'll say, it's important to have a power rating list of all teams involved, whether it be the NFL, NBA or college sports.

Publications such as *The Gold Sheet*, *Sports Reporter*, *Winning Points*, and my own *Moneymaker* have solid power ratings from which you can form your own mathematical base.

Difficulty of Opposition

It amazes me each year how many handicappers fail to realize the importance of a team's "schedule difficulty." A team with a losing record against tough foes is often superior to a team with a winning record against weak opposition. Having a good power-rating base is a key ingredient in following difficulty of opposition for each team. Having a computer to chart these stats is even more important. In college basketball, for example, it would become far too cumbersome to keep track of 150+ teams by hand.

YOU CAN BET ON IT!

On a given college Saturday, some sixty games are played each week in college basketball. I find a computer to be an absolute must in keeping track of points for-against and opposition difficulty in collegiate basketball. The NBA is more uniform from top to bottom along with the NFL; therefore, difficulty of opposition is less important as the season goes along.

Let's assume you are able to place a good mathematical number on each game based on pure stats. Whether you keep your own power ratings or subscribe to someone's service, make sure you can make your own line on each game in advance. With that thought in mind, it is time to turn our attention to the "intangibles," the emotional factors that will have an influence on the mathematical line you now possess.

Revenge

No factor in sport handicapping can be more important or, for that matter, misleading, than the revenge factor. You hear the word everywhere you go in sports betting circles. A certain team needs revenge while another wants to get double revenge. In pro basketball, we get triple and quadruple revenge setups. I'll tell you, it's enough to drive you nuts after awhile!

Please, whatever you do, learn all you can about revenge in football, basketball and, yes, even baseball. Remember this: good teams are more capable of extracting revenge from their opponents than bad teams. Real bad teams just keep getting their brains kicked in! Make note of tough, close losses as well as big blowouts.

College sports are more conducive to revenge than pro sports. The kids in college play for the love of the game. Emotion takes precedence over the calculating style played by the pros. In college football, follow certain coaches (winning ones) who love to get their teams up in revenge situations. In college basketball, the months of February and March present some excellent revenge opportunities in what I call "the second season" as conference teams meet each other for a second time. Whether it is pro or college, decide how much value to give revenge. Take your basic math number (spread) and then add or deduct one, two or three points based on this factor.

Due Factors

What is a due factor? On an individual level, it is akin to a person having a series of good days and then one in which he wishes he'd never gotten out of bed. After a series of bad days, a person can almost bank on having a good day, one in which the rain ends and the sun shines on a spectacular rainbow.

On a team level, this factor applies to a good-bad game(s) scenario. A bad team that plays over its head for a while will invariably come back to earth in the most gruesome of manners. A good team playing below its level will rise to the occasion and destroy its opponent by 30 or more points. As a handicapper, you must know when these reversals of form will most likely happen.

When you suspect such an occurrence, you must alter your mathematical line accordingly. If your numbers tell you that Dallas should be a 7-point favorite over the Giants based on pure math, then you might want to alter that figure (upwards, of course) if Dallas has played below its level in recent weeks.

If the Cowboys have played a few big up games in a row, you might want to lower that seven a few points based on the due factor pointing to a down game. By the way, the Cowboys had lost three of four games heading into the battle with the Giants on January 15, 1994. Were they due to play a good game? You bet they were, and the Cowboys responded with a 44-3 ripping of the Giants.

YOU CAN BET ON IT!

Due factors will keep you in line and away from playing the way John Q. Public sees a game. He usually reacts to the latest results and is usually dead wrong.

There you have it. The best of what it takes to beat the 60 percent barrier against the spread. Make a mathematical number (M) on each game. Now add (+) the intangibles (I) such as revenge and due factors. Take these intangibles and adjust your pure math figure accordingly.

The 60 you achieve after this adjustment will be when you compare your own personal line against the Vegas spread. If your number is close to the Las Vegas line, lay off the game. If you see a big difference, play with confidence. And, by the way: you'll hit that 60 with your formula if you play far more dogs than favorites!

Be content on hitting 60 percent against the spread. Until then, for every six winners you hit out of ten, you'll still miss four games. That is a fact of life. Accept it.

5

PUT YOURSELF IN THE POSITION TO WIN

Whether you bet on sports or gamble on the casino table games, the main purpose of your efforts should be to try to put yourself in the position to win. This sounds very simplistic and obvious. In actuality, it is not. In football betting, for example, many people bet early on Sunday to take a position for the following week's games. This is called handicapping the line. If the number moves up or down a few points, the bettor will wager an equal amount on the other side of the game. Let's say an opening line of -9 favors New England over Dallas. By game time, almost a week later, the point spread has moved to New England -12. This doesn't happen very often, but it's worth being aware of.

Originally, you wagered $110 to win $100 at -9. Once the line moved to -12, you have the chance to "win good," without the risk of "losing bad." You simply bet another $110, but this time you take +12 and bet on Dallas. Now, let's study the different scenarios that could take place.

If New England wins by more than 13, or by less than 8, you lose $10. If Dallas wins the game, you lose $10. In the worst possible situation, you lose only $10. I always like to inform you about the downside of any betting possibility. Now let's look at the upside of this. If New England wins by 10 or 11 points, you would win $200 because you would have New England -9 and Dallas +12.

If New England wins by nine or 12, you would win $100 because you would have pushed (tied) one bet and won the other. This is called "siding" a wager. To get your full value out of this wager, the point spread should vary at least three points. Bottom line: the worst you can do is lose $10. If you want to look at it odds-wise, you are getting up to 20-1 odds on this bet. The larger the point spread differential, the better your chance to cash both sides.

On numerous occasions, I've seen people at the craps table actually give up an advantageous position. The situation consists of a wrong bettor (Don't Pass) making a wager on the come out roll. He bets $25 on the Don't Pass. If the shooter rolls a seven or 11, he loses. If the shooter rolls a two or a 3, he wins. If the shooter rolls a 12, it's a push.

Let's analyze this. There are six ways to make a seven: 1-6, 6-1, 2-5, 5-2, 3-4, 4-3. There are two ways to make an eleven: 6-5 and 5-6. There are eight ways to lose on the come out roll if you are a wrong way bettor. There are two ways to roll a three: 1-2 and 2-1; but only one way to roll a two: 1-1. So there are only three ways to win on the come out roll, making you a big underdog on the initial roll.

Now comes the interesting part. Once a point is established, the wrong way bettor becomes a favorite. How big a favorite depends on the come out roll. If the number is four or 10, the wrong way bettor would become a 2-1 favorite. No one would pick up their wager in this instance.

I have witnessed more than a few people pick up their Don't Pass bets if a six or eight is thrown. Let's say a six is thrown and that is now the point. The bettor is still a 7-6 favorite to win the wager. Instead of picking up their bet, they should have placed a wager of $24 on the 6. If the shooter sevens out, they would win $1: the $25 on the Don't Pass, minus the $24 they would lose on the place bet.

Conversely, if the shooter makes the point by rolling a 6, they would win $28 on the place bet six and lose $25 on the Don't Pass line. After hitting the 6, they should call off their place bet and collect their profit of $3. If you gamble smartly and recognize certain advantages that will make you the favorite, your chances of winning will be greatly enhanced.

CHAPTER
3
PROFESSIONAL PLAYS

1

BETTING OVER/UNDERS

by Sonny Reizner

Over-under betting has grown with amazing rapidity in the past several years. While it was virtually unknown in the 1970s, it is now offered in every sports betting establishment. When totals betting was still relatively new, the sportsbook operators and bookmakers didn't have as good a feel for it as they did for the older and more conventional type of wagering. Now, however, they have it down pat.

A "total," or over-under bet, is simply a number which the house puts up on a game on which the player may bet that the total points scored in that game go over that number or under that number. (In case of a tie, there is no decision and the money wagered is returned to the bettor.) Betting on totals is a relatively new form of wagering on sports that has been increasing in popularity with the sports betting public, but not necessarily with the sports book and bookmakers. The player, in betting totals, has some distinct advantages in this proposition that he does not enjoy in the traditional form of sports betting—choosing one side or the other.

Although the house percentage is the same for both types of wagers (pick either side and lay 11-10), which gives the house an apparent advantage, there are certain built-in factors that give an edge to the player in the totals proposition that are not present when betting one team or another. The betting of totals is an art (or science) by itself, independent of a person's skill at choosing which side will win, and by how much.

For example, if a bettor felt that two traditional rivals would play a hard fought and bitter struggle with both sides hitting hard and yielding ground grudgingly, he might be convinced the game will be an exceptionally low scoring game, and decide to bet the game "under." He might have no opinion at all about which side will win.

I believe that the astute handicapper who devotes most of his handicapping efforts to the totals proposition has a distinct edge over the oddsmaker. Most of the other sportsbook operators I know agree with me. There is evidence for this opinion in the fact that most, if not all, sportsbooks have a lower limit on totals wagering than they do on team wagering.

At the Castaways Sportsbook, which I managed before it closed, we would have a $5,000 or $10,000 limit on team bets, but we would have only a $1,000 limit on overs and unders. There are a number of reasons for this, and they all point to the same conclusion. We, the sportsbooks, are less sure of our ability to post the correct number in the totals proposition than we are in the traditional pointspread proposition. The reasons for this are:

1. We have been putting up numbers on the pointspread proposition for 35 years. The totals proposition is relatively new.

2. We know that when we put up a pointspread number, we will get large plays from many different kinds of bettors. Sure, there will be wise guys who might be getting an edge on some games, but we also get large bets from fans, sportsmen, alumni, TV watchers, etc. Not everyone who places a large bet on the result of a game is a wise guy. In total, however, the average fan or alumnus does not have a rooting interest in how many points are

scored. Most of the big money bets we receive on totals are from sharp players. We know that if we put up a weak totals number, we will be hit hard on one side only.

3. We have only so much time and energy to devote to putting out our numbers. Because there is overwhelmingly more action on "result" betting than there is on over-under betting, most of the time and energy is spent on putting up the right numbers on the teams. Between professional and college football, there are about 50 games each weekend on which we must make a line. There are then about 17 games (14 pro games and three college games—the ones on TV) on which we also put up totals. In basketball on a Saturday, there can be 60 college games, plus nine pro games. We therefore have about 70 games on which we must put out a line, and another 10 or 12 on which we must put out a total. In baseball, we put out a line and total on every game.

Also, there is considerable overlapping of sports. In September and part of October, we have both baseball and football. In April, we have both baseball and basketball. In November, we have both basketball and football.

We put up our totals numbers with whatever time and energy we have left over from our battle with the main proposition, and I would be the first to admit that our totals numbers are not as strong as our pointspread numbers. Assuming there is a general weakness in the totals numbers, how can the player go about exploiting that weakness?

Here is what a serious and dedicated player should know and do to attack the totals proposition:

- Record and study the statistics and the number of points or runs scored between all teams who played against each other, and at which site, plus the number of points scored and allowed by each team against all opponents.

- Look for high numbers and see if you can find a reason to bet under. Look for low numbers and see if you can find a reason to bet over. Analyze the style of play of each team in each game. Are the teams offensive-minded or defensive-minded? Is one team offense-minded and the other defensive-minded?

- Understand the coaching philosophy of each coach and the game plan likely to be employed. Some coaches or managers tend to sit on a lead, while others keep trying to score until the final gun, also called "running it up."

- In football, know if a team's main weapon is the pass or the run. Rushing plays eat up the clock. Many more plays, in the course of a game, will be attempted by passing teams. In basketball, you must know if a team plays run and gun, or attempts to meticulously set up plays. In baseball, you must know if a team likes to sacrifice or swing away.

- Are there defensive injuries that might tend to permit the other team to score more easily?

- Are there offensive injuries that would inhibit scoring?

YOU CAN BET ON IT!

- How important is the game? Very crucial games tend to be low scoring games, because each team plays more conservatively.

- Special occasions: the opening of a new stadium or park, the final career game of a player who has meant a lot to the team, a coach's last game. Occasions such as these seem to motivate a team towards its best effort and a high scoring show.

- Revenge factor: teams which lost by a big margin in a previous encounter with a certain opponent will try to run up the score, if they can, when playing that opponent again.

- Look for an "over" in football, particularly towards the end of a season, when a large margin of victory might be the deciding factor in qualification for a playoff spot.

- Some teams seem to have the ability to nullify the main offensive weapon of certain opponents. This applies to all sports. In football, some teams seem to throttle certain quarterbacks or to shut down particular running backs. In baseball, some pitchers tend to dominate certain hitters. In basketball, a team can have a history of holding a star offensive player, who usually scores lot of points against most teams, to very few.

- If you like a game "over," it is best to wait before getting down.

- If the weather is bad at game time, you might not want to bet it.

• If you like a game "under," bet early. Bad weather can only enhance your chance of winning.

This is by no means a complete list of things to watch for and study in forming an opinion on whether a game will go over or under. These points are presented in order to show you the type of thinking that goes into the decision making of a good over-under player.

Some of the advantages the over-under player enjoys over the sportsbooks are:

1. The quality of the linemakers in putting up totals is less than their quality in putting up pointspread numbers.

2. Totals numbers will move with greater rapidity and with greater variation from place to place than will pointspread numbers. You might find a football game at 48 in one sportsbook and at 46 in another. You might find a baseball game at seven in one place and at six and a half in another. A basketball game could be 232 here and 235 there. If you know your stuff and have properly analyzed a given game, with variations such as those, you should be getting the best of it when you plunk down your money.

3. Many sportsbooks deal totals only because they must do so to remain competitive with other sportsbooks. You might say that totals are the "loss leaders" of the sports book business.

4. Injuries often affect the totals proposition more than the sportsbook adjusts for them. Though the totals number may move upon knowledge of

an injury, it will often not move enough, or may move too much.

5. The astute player has a built-in advantage. He can put more time and effort into handicapping his totals plays than the bookmaker can put into making his totals line.

2

BETTING PROPOSITIONS

by Fred Crespi
Manager of Race & Sportsbook, The Palms Casino Resort

In synchronization with the ever-growing popularity of sports wagering, proposition bets have now found their own niche within the betting community. While the sports player has been used to the basic offers available on various sports like football, basketball, baseball and hockey, the bookmakers have been increasing their efforts in order to offer more of what the player wants.

In this day of sports book and casino competitiveness, the wealth of different wagering options is not only a way for the player to visit your establishment on a more consistent basis, but can often lead to positive publicity for the book and bookmaker alike. Let's dive into exactly what proposition wagers are and the many different facets they encompass.

Proposition wagers, or "props" as they are more commonly called, are simply creative ways to offer more of a wagering variety within a single sport. Prop bets are generally surrounded around individual players and the likelihood or non-likelihood of certain events occurring during the course of a game or a season. For instance, with the great home run race of 1998 between Mark McGwire and Sammy Sosa, individual books followed suit and offered prop bets including both those players.

A specific proposition found during that eventful season involved Mark McGwire and whether he would or wouldn't break the single season home run mark of 61 established by

Roger Maris. That specific proposition may have looked like this:

> Event: Will Mark McGwire break the HR
>   record of 61?
> Bet #: 4201   4202
> Line: Yes -150   No +130

The bet numbers are used for the ticket writer to know what event and side the bettor is interested in, and the 'yes' at −150 signifies that the bookmaker felt that McGwire was a favorite to break the record, asking the bettor to lay $1.50 for every $1.00 they would like to win.

If a bettor believed Maris' record was safe in 1998, they could wager $1.00 on the NO, and win $1.30, for a total payout of $2.30 (bet amount + amount won). A spectacular event or course of events in and around any particular sport will often lead to more and more props being available.

The creativity by the bookmakers is basically limitless. However, while that home run race was indeed a very exciting time for baseball fans and bettors alike, there is really one sport and single event that can be attributed to the increased popularity of proposition wagering. Professional football has always led the way in terms of popularity and interest among sports players, and the Super Bowl only magnifies this.

While game lines, over-under total points and money lines are available on practically every pro football game, the bookmakers really wanted to take the popularity of this sport to another level and create different and unique wagering options for the players. The Super Bowl is at the center of the proposition bet craze, and can easily be attributed as the genesis event of all prop bets.

Some of the more popular prop bets found during the Super Bowl include the following:

- First, second, third and fourth quarter wagering with sides and over-unders.

- Player to score the first touchdown and player to score the last touchdown—each participating team would have anywhere between seven and ten players listed with odds associated to them. For example, Deion Branch (New England) was 8-1 to score the first touchdown in Super Bowl XXXVIII (A $10 bet would win the player $80 for a total return of $90).

- Will either team score in the first six minutes of the game?

- First team to use a coach's challenge.

- Over/Under largest lead of the game by either team.

- Over/Under total fumbles lost and total interceptions by both teams.

- Will there be a special teams touchdown scored by either team?

- Will the game ever be tied after 0-0?

The list can go on and on, as sportsbooks now have as many as 150 different bets on the Super Bowl ranging from individual players props like total completions by a quarterback, total rushing yards by a running back, and total receptions made by various receivers. However, the evolution of proposition wagering hasn't stopped at the basics, as more and more bookmakers now like to use other sports and their outcomes in creating unique prop bets.

For instance, at The Palms Casino Resort in Las Vegas, a fan of English Premier League soccer could have wagered Manchester United goals scored on Super Bowl Sunday against total number of New England Patriot touchdowns, or golf fans could have wagered on Ernie Els' fourth round score at the Johnnie Walker Classic in Bangkok, Thailand against the total rushing yards by Carolina's Stephen Davis. That is how far proposition wagering has come, and as long as bookmakers have an imagination, more and more unique props will continue to be available. While football proposition bets are the most prominent, that hasn't diminished the bookmaker's enthusiasm in creating a variety of other betting options in sports like baseball, basketball, hockey, golf, soccer, and auto racing. As the popularity of the sport and its players increase, the demand for proposition bets also increases.

The National Basketball Association is a perfect example of this, as the league has been flooded with great young talents like Kevin Garnett, Kobe Bryant, and most recently Carmelo Anthony and the phenom of all phenoms, LeBron James. Bookmakers wasted no time in offering a wide range of prop bets surrounding James, including the very creative Michael Jordan rookie year point average versus James' rookie point average. With Jordan's average of 28.2 points per game in 1984-85, bookmakers ranged anywhere from Jordan –12.5 points per game to –13 over LeBron's projected average of 16 points per game in his rookie season. Other unique props include an over/under on LeBron's most points scored in any one game during the season, and whether or not he could lead his team, the Cleveland Cavaliers, to the playoffs in his rookie season.

Major League Baseball ranks neck and neck with pro basketball as far as variety offered in terms of proposition wagers. This can be attributed to the popularity of the game in terms of a fantasy appeal and the wealth of statistics kept for batters and pitchers alike. Bettors can expect to be able to wager on the player to finish with the most home runs, or pitcher to finish with the most wins on a yearly basis. Individual player props are also widely available, ranging from over-unders on total number of home runs hit, to total batting average, to total bases for the entire year, to total number of strikeouts by individual pitchers. Bookmakers will generally use the most popular players, and players who are on the verge of career or seasonal milestones. Fans will soon be able to wager on whether or not Barry Bonds will break Hank Aaron's all time home run record of 755, and most likely a before or after date range of when 756 will fly. It would also not be a stretch to see a proposition like this one:

When Barry Bonds hits home run number 756, will it land in McCovey Cove?

Yes +500

No -700

(Note: McCovey Cove is the body of water named after Willie McCovey behind the right field stands at Pacific Bell Park in San Francisco. The home run must land in the water to be graded as Yes. If Barry Bonds does not break the record, bets will be refunded.)

This is only an example of course, as is the disclaimer below the proposition, but this is just the type of creativity that can be expected in this day and age out of many bookmakers. Following pro football, pro basketball, and pro baseball, props can also be found in less high volume wagering sports like hockey, golf and auto racing.

YOU CAN BET ON IT!

Sportsbooks are always looking to cater to players who enjoy the less high profile sports, and what better way to do that than offer a wide range of proposition bets? Numerous props are found during the hockey Stanley Cup Finals, including goal differential props, player points and assists props or goalie save props. Golf propositions are offered on a weekly basis in terms of individual matchup props, pitting one golfers stroke total versus another, and the menu only increases during the week of a major tournament like The Masters or the U.S. Open. Prior to those events, bookmakers are hard at work coming up with whether or not individual golfers will make the second round cut, and over-unders on first round scores. Other popular golf props included whether or not there will be a playoff, or whether or not there will be a hole in one during any of the four days.

Like golf, auto racing has also picked up in popularity in terms of wagering, with the focus of that centering on NASCAR and the Nextel Cup Series. Popular drivers like Dale Earnhardt Jr., Jeff Gordon and Jimmie Johnson can usually be found on a weekly basis paired up against each other, and much like the golf major tournaments, the prop menu really picks up when the series hits the Las Vegas Motor Speedway on an annual basis. Propositions including total number of caution flags, total number of cars finishing on the lead lap, best finish among teammates, and winning car number props can be readily available at numerous sportsbooks.

Only a lack of imagination can curtail the prop menu, and that is simply something oddsmakers do not lack in this day and age. This is a great time as far as various options for the sports player, and proposition wagering is a large reason for that. As the demand continues to grow, properties like the Palms Casino Resort will continue to put in the effort and time needed to give the sports bettors all the different wagering options they deserve.

3

BETTING PARLAYS

by Bill Brown

Parlay cards... teasers... mega teasers!

Bring parlay cards up in conversation and you'll quickly hear, "Sucker bets!" Ask one of the many sports talk show hosts their opinion: "Sucker bets!"

Read about them in a sports publication: "Sucker bets!" Ask the wise guys of the business: "Sucker bets!" Ask the sportsbook personnel: "Sucker bets!"

Ask almost anybody: "If you're going to play them, play them strictly as a fun bet and don't use your serious gambling money." Well, I'm here to tell you that as much as I respect the sports and handicapping knowledge of these people, many of whom are associates and friends of mine, their opinion may be wrong.

Does this mean I am an advocate of playing parlay cards? I'm going to temporarily hedge my answer and say, "Not necessarily!" Ask a gambler what the odds are of hitting a three-team parlay and the usual answer is one out of eight. Ask him what the odds are of hitting a five-team parlay and the usual answer is 1 out of 32.

How does he arrive at these answers; are they even correct? If the payoff is 25 for 1, is playing a five-team parlay a good bet? Not if the odds of hitting all five is 1 out of 32! The question I have is whether or not the odds are actually 1 out of 32. Most of us understand how to calculate the probability of a mathematical occurrence, at least on some of the simpler questions. However, just to make sure, a short lesson in calculating probability is about to be given.

YOU CAN BET ON IT!

What are the odds of flipping a coin and having it come up heads? Since the result of flipping a normal coin can only be a head or a tail, we have only two possible results. We are looking for a head to occur, one of the two possible results; therefore the odds of a heads occurring is 1 out of 2, 50-50, 1-1 or 1/2. Now get out a coin and flip it ten times. Does it come out exactly five heads and five tails?

Most of the time it will not. Suppose it comes up three heads and seven tails. Does this mean we are wrong in our thinking that the odds of heads occurring is 1 out of 2? Of course not.

This simply means that when you make a small sampling of only ten flips, the end result may not follow the true odds. However, if you flip a coin two million times, the results will come within a very small percentage of the actual mathematical odds. In other words, the more samplings you make of an event, the closer the results will come to the true odds of that event. When you look for two consecutive events occurring, you must multiply the odds of the first event happening times the odds of the second event happening. And therefore, the odds of your coin coming up heads twice in a row are 1-2 x 1-2, which is 1-4 or 1 out of 4. The odds of your coin coming up heads three times in a row are 1-2 x 1-2 x 1-2, which is 1-8 or 1 out of 8.

If you were allowed to make a wager on your flipping heads five times in a row, would you make it if someone would give you 28-1 odds on your wager? Probably not, since you are not getting a fair return considering the actual odds of 31-1 (the same as saying 1 out of 32).

What if they would give you 40-1 odds? Would you now make the bet? The answer should be yes since you now have an "overlay"—that is, the payoff odds is greater than the actual mathematical odds of winning. Although the actual odds of an event is greatly against you (five heads in a row is 1 out of 32), so long as you have an overlay, the bet is a good one, especially if you are given a chance to make the same wager a large number of times.

Ask a knowledgeable horse handicapper if he would bet on a 5-1 shot (according to his calculations) if the tote board showed it going off at 8-1. Playing parlay cards can be compared to this same situation. The chart that follows this column represents your chances of hitting a parlay card based on how good you believe you are.

For example, the odds of picking six out of six when you normally win at a 58 percent rate are 1 out of 26. The odds of picking 10 out of 10 and winning $X for a $5 wager at one of the local betting establishments who offers such a card is one out of 232, if you are one of the very few who picks winners at a 58 percent rate.

What is interesting is that if you can pick winners at 54 percent or better on a typical parlay card, you will have created an overlay—that is, the payoff is greater than the odds of hitting that winning combination. For example, a typical 6-team parlay may pay 40-1. However, a parlay bettor who picks at a 56 percent winning rate has one chance out of 32 (31-1) of hitting all 6 out of 6. His skill has created an overlay condition. Does that mean I'm suggesting he plays parlay cards instead of straight bets?

Not necessarily. What I am suggesting is that parlay cards may not be as bad a bet as we have been told. For the occasional visitor to Las Vegas (or even a local) who cannot make (or does not have the money to make) a large number of straight bets, which one may have to do to win a considerable amount of money, a parlay card may make sense.

In addition, there is no law against making straight bets and parlay card wagers, so why not set aside a small part of your bankroll for an occasional parlay ticket, even if you are a professional handicapper?

YOU CAN BET ON IT!

The payoff chart shown on the following page is a common one that may be found during football season. You can use the same "odds of hitting" for any parlay card, including teasers and mega-teasers. The overlay conditions for those cards will be when the payoff odds are greater than your "odds of hitting." For example, if a 5-team teaser pays 6-1, look at the 5-team column and go down until you find a number less than 6. In this example, you have to be picking teasers at 70 percent or better to have an overlay condition. If your records show you've been picking at this rate or better on your teaser plays, a 5-team teaser may be an acceptable play.

Typical Payoff Amount and Number of Picks

Winning %	2.8-1	6-1	11-1	20-1	40-1	80-1	150-1	300-1	800-
40	6.25	15.6	39.1	98	244	610	1526	3815	953?
42	5.67	13.5	32.4	77	182	434	1033	2459	585.
44	5.17	11.7	26.7	61	138	313	712	1618	367?
46	4.73	10.3	22.3	49	105	229	499	1084	235?
48	4.34	9.0	18.8	39	82	170	355	739	154(
50	4.00	8.0	16.0	32	64	128	256	512	102∙
52	3.70	7.1	13.7	26.3	51	97	187	360	692
54	3.43	6.4	11.8	21.8	40	75	138	256	474
56	3.19	5.7	10.2	18.2	32	58	103	185	330
58	2.97	5.1	8.8	15.2	26	45	78	135	232
60	2.78	4.6	7.7	12.9	21.4	36	60	99	165
62	2.60	4.2	6.8	10.9	17.6	28	46	74	119
64	2.44	3.8	6.0	9.3	14.6	22.7	35.5	56	87
66	2.30	3.5	5.3	8.0	12.1	18.3	27.8	42	64
68	2.16	3.2	4.7	6.9	10.1	14.9	21.9	32.2	47.?
70	2.04	2.9	4.2	5.9	8.5	12.1	17.4	24.8	35.∙
72	1.93	2.7	3.7	5.2	7.2	10.0	13.9	19.2	26.?
74	1.83	2.5	3.3	4.5	6.1	8.2	11.1	15.0	20.?
76	1.73	2.3	3.0	3.9	5.2	6.8	9.0	11.8	15.(
78	1.64	2.1	2.7	3.5	4.4	5.7	7.3	9.4	12.(
80	1.56	1.95	2.4	3.1	3.8	4.8	6.0	7.5	9.3∙
82	1.49	1.81	2.21	2.70	3.3	4.0	4.9	6.0	7.3∙
84	1.42	1.69	2.01	2.39	2.9	3.4	4.0	4.8	5.7
86	1.35	1.57	1.83	2.13	2.5	2.9	3.3	3.9	4.5
88	1.29	1.47	1.67	1.89	2.2	2.5	2.8	3.2	3.6
90	1.23	1.37	1.52	1.69	1.9	2.1	2.3	2.6	2.9

CHAPTER 4
BEATING THE GAMES

1

ELEMENT X

by Mort Olshan
Editor & Publisher, *The Gold Sheet*

If you think betting on football is a walk in the park, you're likely to end up getting mugged. But after nearly fifty years as a sports handicapper, I can tell you, "Don't be deceived." Winning just over half of your bets isn't nearly as scary as it sounds.

Experts who have been around the block a few times know why upwards of 90 percent of those challenging the pointspread on a regular basis are losers on a regular basis. In football, there is a variable we commonly refer to as Element X. Element X is a built-in efficiency (or deficiency) factor that encompasses all the unpredictable situations that generally occur after the kickoff, including blocked punts, intercepted passes, fumbles, key injuries, critical penalties, teams playing over their heads or beneath their potential, deflected passes that are either caught or intercepted, and first-down measurements decided by inches. These elements are totally unpredictable, and opinions vary as to how they affect the pointspread.

We once traveled to Las Vegas to interview several of the best-known figures in the sports betting world. We asked them what percentage of the games they thought were decided by Element X.

The consensus of these Las Vegas experts was that at least 50 percent of all games played during any football season are decided by one of the aforementioned factors or something related to them.

Let's assume that the average football bettor makes 100 bets this season. And let us further hypothesize that 50 percent of those bets will be decided by impossible-to-predict factors. That translates into 25 winners and 25 losers decided by Element X.

Now let us assume that the other 50 games are relatively predictable, and through hard work and research our bettor is able to accurately forecast an impressive 35 winners and 15 losers, or 70 percent. Adding the 25 winners from the unpredictable situations to the 35 winners from the predictable category, we find our bettor winding up with a 60 percent winning average.

And before you scoff at 60 percent, you should realize this: if you started the season with a $3,000 bankroll and picked winners 60 percent of the time, even if you bet as little as $100 per game, you would end up with a profit of $1,600 (60 winners x $100 minus 40 losers x $110). That's a return on investment of 53 percent.

You would be hard-pressed to find another investment with that rate of return. And if you had bet $200 per game over those 100 games, winning 60 games would net you $3,200, which is a 107 percent return on investment.

So don't believe the fraudulent claims of charlatans quoting 70 and 80 percent. If you want to be a winner at betting football, this is the reality.

2

GETTING AN
EXTRA ANGLE

How you watch a game is very important. You can win a bet without wagering—it's all in the preparation. In fact, watching a football game without a bet can sometimes be to your advantage.

Often, when you bet on a game, you have a tendency to be very prejudiced towards the team you bet on. Let's say, for example, that you bet on the 49ers against the Rams. When the 49ers receive the ball on the opening kickoff, what are you looking for? Obviously you want the 49ers to have a great kickoff return.

If the 49ers only return the ball to the 15-yard line, is it because of the poor blocking, or the good coverage? Are you noticing what the Rams are doing, or are they just an obstacle in the way of winning your bet?

Do you concentrate solely on the 49ers on offense, or do you give equal attention to the Rams on defense? If there is a fumble or interception, do you curse your horrible luck, or do you make a mental note of the defensive alignment the Rams were in? Next week, when the Rams are playing, this piece of information could be critical to your handicapping evaluation.

Many of the astute handicappers in Las Vegas like to videotape games they watch. When the outcome is still in doubt, we often get caught up in the action. The excitement of the two-minute drill and the tension of whether your team will cover the spread will exhaust your memory of the preceding part of the game.

After the game, if you taped it, you can review it at your leisure and concentrate on the fundamentals. It's amazing how much information you miss when you are watching the game live. Many times, the big play occurs because of the seemingly insignificant plays that occurred before it. When you are viewing the game live, you have a tendency to forget about those plays.

Another good tip is to keep a log on how a coach calls a game. For over-under bettors, this is extremely important. If you know a coach likes to bleed the clock with a lead, and if the total seems high, this piece of information might just put you on the right side. Conversely, if a coach is always playing to score points, no matter what the score is, you might want to at least consider the over.

This is particularly true in college football. The coaches are very aware of the polls. They are voted on and are closely watched by alumni, students, and fans. The coaches often say that the polls are meaningless, but in fact their salaries and tenure are often measured by their national rankings.

Another thing to look for and keep in your memory bank is how long the starting backfield stays in the game. Different coaches have different coaching philosophies. If you are a totals bettor, it is critical to your bankroll to be aware of the tendencies of the coach.

An additional way to get an edge in handicapping is to attend a sporting event. When you do this, you are not reliant on what the camera reveals to you. If you want to concentrate on the line play, invest in a good pair of binoculars so that you can follow the blocking very closely.

Also, in the latter stages of the game, you can focus on the intensity and freshness of their play. Are they holding their blocks in the fourth quarter as well as they did in the first quarter? Many times, the same tendencies you see in one game will be repeated over and over again during the season.

YOU CAN BET ON IT!

If you attend a game that is televised, be sure to tape it because there are many distractions at the ballpark: people standing up, vendors in the way, and so on. Remember, you are trying to gain an edge in your handicapping capability. Each small piece of information, no matter how seemingly insignificant, will add up over time to present you with a much clearer picture to handicap.

Each sport offers the bettor a completely different set of circumstances. One thing I stress is to keep a watchful eye on the defense. Defense not only helps to win games, but more importantly to the sports bettor, defense helps to win wagers!

3

WIN WITH PATIENCE

A certain air of expectancy fans the winds of football season. Clipboards that have been collecting dust since January are being broken out. Although the weather screams summer, there is a faint whisper that keeps getting louder. Ever so insistently, the voice of the not too distant future says, "Football season is coming."

Football bettors live for September. Not because of the change of seasons that provides relief from the incessant heat, but rather because the game they love to bet on and analyze returns to seduce and haunt them. To sports bettors, football season is equivalent to a fresh pot of coffee in the morning. It's time to wake up and get back into action. In Las Vegas and throughout the country, football is the king in betting circles. Many people who never think of wagering on baseball or basketball emerge from their hibernation with a fresh bankroll, frothing at the mouth at the mere mention of a point spread.

A word to the wise: take it easy! Football season is long and requires patience and persistence to endure. Do yourself a favor and bet in percentages rather than amounts. Let's say you begin the season with $1,000. Bet five percent ($50 a game) to begin with. If you're winning, the five percent you wager will represent more money as time goes by.

For example, if you build up your bankroll to $1,500, your five percent will now be a $75 bet. Conversely, if you're losing, your five percent wager will be scaled down to a lesser amount. The old axiom, "bet less when losing and more when winning," will take care of itself using the percentage method. Several aspects involved in handicapping a game are worth exploring. First off is the home field advantage. An over-used and much accepted rule of thumb is that the home field is worth three points. Well, sometimes it is and sometimes it isn't.

In my opinion, playing the Denver Broncos in Denver is a lot tougher than playing the Chargers in San Diego. And how about playing the New England Patriots at home? Get my point? When a rule of thumb is applied to football, it is usually just a lazy man's way to handicap. Each field is different to it's home team. Do your homework and adjust your power ratings accordingly.

Secondly, most people bet the favorites and most people lose. Keep a close eye on the "dogs" and don't be afraid to go against popular opinion. When the guys get together Sunday night and cry in their beers ("How could they possibly have lost?!"), you can buy the next round with your winnings.

Thirdly, the lines don't vary nowadays as much as they used to, but they still vary enough to make it worth your while to shop around. What may seem to be an insignificant difference on the surface will add up to your advantage over the long run of the football season.

Finally, unless you've been hiding you can't help but notice the advertisements for a bunch of football contests. It all started many years ago when a visionary named Sonny Reizner initiated a contest at the gone-but-not-forgotten Castaways "Hole-in-the-Wall" sportsbook. Today, almost every sportsbook in Las Vegas offers some type of contest. You can win lots of money or cars, even a house.

Most contests reward you for picking the most winners, but a few also give grand prizes for the most losers and for those who get closest to picking 50 percent. Check out all the contests and read the fine print to choose the one that best applies to your skills and bankroll.

4

TOOLS OF THE TRADE

You work to strengthen your weakest link, not to worry about the strongest one.

-- Bum Phillips

"There's something happenin' here; what it is ain't exactly clear." So the song goes. What's happening is football season. Football bettors are like hibernating bears. All spring and summer they dwell in a semi-conscious state until football season arrives. Then they awaken, armed with fistfuls of cash, ready to do battle with the bookmakers.

But before embarking on your long football season journey, filled with excitement and sweat, I strongly suggest you take a moment of personal evaluation to figure out what you can afford to wager. As famed sports bettor Lem Banker would say, "Bet not what you want to win, but what you can afford to lose."

A betting situation that almost everybody comes across during the season is known by many names, but its common moniker is the lock. Beware of anyone who utters this word prior to any sporting event. The only locks you can count on are found in the deli and are spelled differently!

If someone insists that his lock is a sure thing and backs up his opinion with point spreads and line movements that seem to clarify his position, do yourself a favor: either don't bet the game or bet exactly the opposite of his advice.

A few good plays pop up each year. In the past, the standard was the Monday night home team that is an underdog. From 1969 to 1990, the home team "dog" was 42-17 against the spread. From 1985 to 1990, the record was

20-6. This wager was the king of the no-brainers. During this time, if you simply bet the Monday night home team underdog, you would have done extremely well. Although there are no locks and no sure things, this was about as close, percentage-wise, as you can get.

A couple of tools that will help you in your quest for finding winners are *The Gold Sheet* and *The Point Spread Playbook*. *The Gold Sheet* is known as the "Bible of Football Bettors."

You'll often see handicappers referring to it prior to placing their wagers in the sportsbooks of Las Vegas. Founded in 1957, it sets the standard in the industry with its up-to-the-minute statistics, injury reports and power ratings that many bookmakers use as their essential guide to setting their lines.

The late *Gold Sheet* publisher Mort Olshan lived by a code of honesty and integrity, and believed he could "make a difference." I enjoy the newsletter's easy-to-read and understand format. The power ratings are of tremendous value in comparing teams. The *Gold Sheet* continues under the tutelage of Gary Olshan, Mort's son and the excellent staff that has been there for years, including Chuck Sippl, Bruce Marshall, etc.

Another interesting and informative tool of the sports bettor is *The Point Spread Playbook* by Al O'Donnell. This book highlights each NFL team with past performance charts which include point spreads and over-unders. It evaluates trends and tendencies of each team like no other publication on the market.

Al O'Donnell backs up his picks with his own cash. I like that! His book gets a very high grade on accuracy and is easy to understand. *The Point Spread Playbook* should be near the armchair of everyone who wagers on professional ports. It also comes with a money back guarantee, and can be reached by calling 847-398-7508.

The football season is a long one so don't go overboard on any one game. Relax—keep your wits about you—a lot of emotion will be riding on your bets from week to week. Try to separate your feelings from your statistics. Why bet your home team just because you are a fan? And don't believe everything you read in a local newspaper about its home team, because they are often too close to the team to be thoroughly objective. Rely on many different sources for your handicapping.

The best advice of all is the old saying, "Bet with your head, not over it."

5

GETTING A FEEL
FOR THE ACTION

I've always believed that you can think positive just as well as you can think negative.

-- Sugar Ray Robinson

We think in generalities, we live in detail.

-- Alfred North Whitehead

The late Sonny Reizner put it succinctly when he spoke of the true essence of a successful sports bettor: "They have to have feel." Opportunities arise that you have to recognize, have to feel, to become a winner. Many times, these situations are very subtle and the novice won't understand them. But the wily betting veteran jumps all over them!

In all sports there are certain spots that the top handicappers lie in wait for. Some are psychological, others are scheduling factors. For example, take a team that had a terrible record the previous year in pro football. They're lagging in season ticket sales and they're playing a team that made the playoffs the year before. The coach of the opposing team has traditionally used the pre-season for trying out new players, hardly playing any starters past the first quarter. In an interview, the coach has said that he could care less about winning during the pre-season. Often times, the team that has something to prove, will prove something. Often times, but not always.

In college football, having a feel for a team's history and how that might influence them in relation to their on-field performance on any given Saturday is extremely important. Many college coaches have said that they can get the maximum effort from their squads only three or four times per season.

The question is, "How does the handicapper recognize these situations before they occur?" And maybe more importantly, "How do you take advantage of them?"

Obviously, if you are successful at recognizing these factors and a myriad of others, you just might be one of the few who can consistently beat sports betting.

Of course, the oddsmaker takes such factors as weather and playing surface into consideration before he sets the line. No matter how good you are, it's always a battle. One of the advantages bettors have is that they get to choose which games they want to bet on. The bookmaker may put up more than sixty games in a weekend. Pick and choose wisely. Just because a game is on television doesn't mean you have to bet on it. (I know that last comment has fallen on many a deaf ear!)

Only you can decide how much to wager. Do yourselves a big favor and don't bet amounts that make you lose control. Lem Banker, a very successful Las Vegas sports bettor says, "Don't bet what you want to win; bet what you can afford to lose!" Lem suggests that you put aside a reasonable amount of money for your playing bankroll. Do not exceed the amount which you determined at the beginning of the season was comfortable for you. Never wager more than eight percent of your bankroll on any one game, no matter how good it looks.

Handicapping sports is an enigma. It looks really easy to win, but it is very tough to beat. If you acquire a feel for the action, you are giving yourself a better chance to be on the plus side at the end of the season.

6

PICKING WINNERS

Nothing like the crack of the bat, the taste of a hot dog and the sweet beginning of yet another baseball season! On the first day, all the teams start out even, giving new birth to a statistical avalanche that will soon begin rolling. Union strikes, lockouts and contract negotiations aside, baseball is a place to come home to.

The heart of a young child beats inside many adults. Baseball is a sanctuary within the soul; springtime is its alarm clock. And to many of us, it is, and always will be, our national pastime. But this is about betting and waxing poetic isn't going to help anyone cash a ticket.

Betting baseball offers the gambler an onslaught of daily propositions that can boggle and thrill the handicapper. To the uninitiated, let me offer some advice. Because there are many games daily, don't go overboard. Neither you nor your bankroll can survive an impetuous thrill-seeking start. You wouldn't begin a marathon sprinting, would you? When you select foods at a buffet, you have to choose what pleases you because you can't eat everything.

It's the same with baseball: you must pick and choose. Find a game you have confidence in. Handicap, study the box scores and injury lists, and then observe your team in action. Find a particular spot you feel is to your advantage.

In almost all cases, baseball has a money line rather than a run line. A money line requires the bettor to just pick the team that's going to win.

Obviously, when a line is set, all aspects of the contest are considered—the lineups, relief pitchers, playing surface, schedule, etc. But most of all, it's the opposing starting pitchers that affect the betting line. That's why they're listed.

If you've watched baseball for years but haven't yet wagered on it, let me explain how the line is established, how you read it and how to bet it. The money line is based on a $100 wager or fraction thereof.

Let's say you see the Dodgers at -$145 against the Cubs at +$135. That means that, if you think the Dodgers will win, you have to bet $145 to win $100. So if you win, you get back the original $145 you wagered, plus the $100 you won. If you like the Cubs, you bet $100 to win an additional $135. In this case, you get back your original $100, plus the $135 you won. That's all there is to it. (Different sportsbooks offer different odds, so the sharp gambler will shop around to find the best number.)

The beauty of betting baseball is that all you have to do is pick the winner. Unlike basketball and football, there are no point spreads to be concerned with. Sounds easy, doesn't it? It's not! Take my word for it, it's tough. However, many successful handicappers do their best during baseball season, for several reasons.

First of all, trends become apparent in baseball that bettors can use to their advantage. The most obvious one is the streak. Bettors can take advantage of both winning and losing streaks. Generally, a streak begins after a team wins or loses three games in a row. The fourth game is when the bettor would be inclined to make a wager. Stay on the streak until the pattern is broken.

Also, certain pitchers have developed patterns over the years. Warm weather pitchers are usually terrible at the beginning of the season. Normally, they will hit their stride in June, July and August.

Baseball has become a game of specialists. The reliever, pinch hitters and glove men all offer a challenge to the handicapper in the late innings. The more you know about a team, the better prepared you'll be to bet into the line. Keep records that pertain to your gambling angle and check out *USA Today* for updated statistics.

Baseball offers many betting opportunities. You can bet on the spring training games, although I advise against it in most cases. The bettor just doesn't know any of the players yet or how long a pitcher will stay in. Betting into the unknown is never a good idea. If you are thinking that gambling is betting into the unknown, you're right. But you usually have a reasonable expectation level.

In spring training, players are trying out for the team, veterans are getting into shape, and no one is yet playing to their abilities. If you want to gamble on a spring training game, do it for a nominal amount and do it for fun. Don't get serious, because spring training is not the time to bet. Many future wagers are also available during the baseball season. Oftentimes, a sharp handicapper who follows baseball can find a spot to take advantage of. I think the total regular season wins proposition offers this opportunity because you can bet either over or under the total that is posted. Of course, you have to lay 11-10 and the sportsbook holds your money for around seven months. That aside, you still might see something that makes sense to you.

Another good suggestion is to put aside the money you can afford to lose as your betting bankroll. Bet only three percent to five percent of it on any one game. That way, you'll survive the down streaks. And when you're winning, you will naturally wager more because you'll have a larger bankroll.

The fascinating game of baseball offers many statistical nuances on a daily basis. Some you can take advantage of; others will take advantage of you. It takes a shrewd bettor to know the difference!

7

BETTING ON THE RUN LINE

by Andrew Iskoe

Betting on games is not hard work. Betting on more winners than losers is hard work.

-- Sonny Reizner

For most of the first half of the twentieth century, betting on baseball dwarfed betting on football, basketball and all other sports. It was the introduction of the pointspread that popularized betting on football, and the general growth in the popularity of the sport further enhanced its growth in betting popularity to the point that, today, football is the king of the sports betting world.

Baseball had declined sharply as a favorite of sports bettors, but in recent years has enjoyed a nice resurgence. Part of the reason baseball betting declined was because, in the modern era, the way of betting on baseball was not as well understood as the way to bet on football and basketball.

In football and basketball, the use of the pointspread in an attempt to equate the abilities of two teams is well understood.

The method of betting, laying a flat 11-10 on either side, has been a standard method of betting for years. All the bettor had to do was to determine whether the favorite looked attractive laying the points, or whether the underdog was appealing plus the points. In baseball, the means of wagering is simple, yet complex.

YOU CAN BET ON IT!

All you have to do in baseball is pick the winner of the game. No pointspreads; just the winner of the game on the field. Period. The complexity comes into play in considering the amount that is required to risk, if you are backing the favorite, or the amount to be won if you back the underdog.

Obviously, not all teams have the same chance of winning, so to lay a flat 11-10 would not be appropriate. Thus, the Money Line is used to equate a team's chances of winning a specific game. In some cases, you may have to lay $180 to $100 to back a huge favorite. Or an underdog may be priced at +$160 to win straight up.

The Money Line really isn't all that difficult a concept to grasp, but because the public is used to thinking in terms of pointspreads for football and basketball, the idea of a Money Line represents foreign thinking.

In reality, all a Money Line represents is a conversion from a team's theoretical percentage of winning into odds to a dollar. A team that is given a 60 percent chance of winning would be favored at -$1.50. A team priced at -$2.00 has a 66.7 percent chance of winning. Over the years, this form of Money Line betting on baseball has been standard.

Sportsbooks make their profits when the underdogs win (which occurs 43-47 percent of the time, excluding pick'em games, as a rule). That is because, in the case of a $1.40 favorite, for example, the backers of the underdog get paid $1.30 for each $1.00, while those who backed the favorite had to put up $1.40 for $1.00 they had hoped to win.

This is based on what is commonly referred to as a "10-cents line," where the difference for most lines is 10 cents between the lay price on favorites and the take price on underdogs. As the price on the favorite gets higher, the difference between favorite and underdog prices rises to 15 or 20 cents (usually at a break point of $1.50, $2.00, etc.)

With that serving as a background to traditional baseball betting, we can now proceed to an area of baseball betting that has many similarities to the pointspread concept that is used in football and basketball. The Run Line is a method of wagering whereby you give up a run and a half to back favorites, or you can take a run and a half with the underdog.

The Run Line serves the same function as a pointspread, where the final score is adjusted by a run and a half in the direction of how the game was bet. For example, a typical Run Line might involve a favorite laying one and a half runs at what is an underdog price, while the true game underdog might have to lay the price at getting one and a half runs. Here's how it might look at a typical sportsbook:

> Philadelphia +1.20 +1 1/2 -1.85
> Cincinnati -1.30 -1 1/2 +1.65

If you thought Philadelphia would win the game, you'd put up $100 to win $120, while to back the Reds, you'd put up $130 to win $100 (on what's known as a "10-cents line"). On the other hand, if you wanted protection against the Reds winning a one run game, you could take the Phils plus one and a half runs, but you would have to lay $185 to win $100. If you felt the Reds should win this game easily, by more than a run, you could bet $100 to win $165. It is not uncommon for a 10-cents line to be used on the "straight" wagers, and a 20-cents line to be used for the Run Line.

The relationship in our example is within the normal range, whereby there could be from a 70 to 95 cents variation between the straight home favorite lay price and the price you get on them as an underdog laying the run and a half. The spread on road favorites is somewhat less (about a 45 to 65 cents spread), since the road team does get to bat in the ninth inning even when leading.

Is the Run Line a good bet? When the favorite wins the game, there is a better than two-in-three chance that they won by more than one run, meaning that laying the run and a half would have produced a winning ticket.

In doing further research into this subject, it appeared clear that taking a run and a half with the underdog was not a favorable proposition. It would seem to be obvious that when you take the run and a half, you have only one situation that wins for you, as opposed to playing the underdog straight—when the favorite wins, but by just one run. When the favorite wins by two or more, your ticket on the dog plus the run and a half is a loser. And when the underdog wins the game outright, you didn't need the run and a half.

When you take the run and a half on the underdog, you are converting what is an underdog price into a favorite price just to get the protection of one extra run. While there can be a case made for a road underdog to take the run and a half to protect against a ninth inning or extra inning loss in breaking a tie game (usually ending in a one run decision), those occurrences happen too infrequently to justify turning an underdog into a favorite. Only in about one of six games does the favorite win by exactly one run.

Laying the run and a half with the favorite is a much-preferred course of action as you convert a favorite into an underdog. You should pay close attention to the price you get on the favorite minus the run and a half to ensure that, over the course of a season, you show a profit.

Using a little basic math, we can work out what that price should be, based upon the facts as outlined above. To simplify matters, let's assume that 55 percent of the time, the favorite wins the game straight up and that 45 percent of the time they lose. Of the 55 percent of the time they win, they win by more than a run 70 percent of the time, and in 30 percent of those games, they win by exactly one run. Thus, over 1,000 games, you'd see the favorite winning 385 games by more than a run, 165 games by one run exactly, and losing 450 games outright.

Let's further simplify matters by assuming that in all games when you lay a run and a half, you do so by laying no more than even money. Often, high priced favorites (as in the case of a team laying -$2.00 straight up), you might be required to lay -$1.10 or -$1.15. But we'll keep it simple without distorting the results of our example.

In the 450 straight up losses, you'd lose $45,000 playing $100 per game. You'd lose an additional $16,500 when the favorite wins by exactly one run. That's a total loss of $61,500, which we can use to get the "break even" underdog price in the 385 games the favorite wins by more than one run. Dividing $61,500 by 385, we get approximately $1.60 as the price we need to take, laying the run and a half, to break even. There are many games where the take back price exceeds +$1.60, when the favorite lays the run and a half.

But let's also compare laying the run and a half to what happens when you make a straight play. In the 550 games that are won straight up by the favorite, regardless of the margin, you'd collect $55,000. In order to break even, you could afford to lose no more than that same amount over the 450 games that the underdog wins.

Dividing the $55,000 by 450, we get an average lay price of just $1.22. So, if these percentages hold up in the future, we are at a disadvantage laying more than -$1.22 on a favorite, and have an advantage laying a run and a half with the favorite when we can get back better than +$1.60. You can do similar math to determine the proper prices for taking the run and a half with the underdog. Again, the only time that +1 1/2 comes into play is when the favorite wins by exactly one run—about 30 percent of the time that the favorite wins.

The math works out to a break even lay price on taking the run and a half of -$1.60 compared to a break even underdog price straight up of +$1.22, obviously the reverse of the same numbers we got when we did the analysis from the other side. Often, to take the run and a half, you'll be laying in excess of -$1.60, while your straight up underdog price is often in excess of +$1.22.

Thus, it would appear to be the best course of action to play underdogs straight up at a price of better than +$1.22 and to lay the run and a half with the favorite at a price of +$1.60 or better, in general. Of course, your own handicapping of games will often justify laying the run and a half at a price of less than +$1.60, but what I wanted to present was the overall, general situation.

By the way, most sportsbooks use the same rules for run line wagers that they do for totals—the game must go eight and a half innings or more when the home team is ahead, or nine innings when the visitor leads. Games that are called after seven innings, for example, result in "No Action," even though, for other purposes, the game is "official" and counts in the standings.

While this has been a relatively elementary presentation of the Run Line and its place in betting major league baseball, I hope that you have been able to grasp some of the more basic concepts, especially the realization that laying the run and a half with the favorite can give you a positive expectation in many situations.

It's somewhat analogous to football in that, in most cases, the pointspread doesn't matter. Just pick the winner of favorite at an underdog price and just giving up one situation: a one run win by the favorite!

In all other situations, you come out ahead—by winning more when the favorite wins by two runs or more—and by losing less in those games the favorites lose outright (by laying just even money rather than a favorite's price). With that, I'll wish you the best of baseball success!

8

A VISIT TO
BAD BEAT CITY

There's no success like failure and failure is no success at all.

-- Bob Dylan

Those of us who gamble have visited this place. Tales abound that are at once unbelievable and as close to near-death experiences as one can possibly imagine. The place I am referring is not Hell, but up the road. The name of this town is Bad Beat.

A while back, I had the reluctant misfortune to visit Bad Beat. I didn't go through the outskirts, but plunged right into the inner city. Just to acquaint you with the place, on the ride into town are the familiar sights of Last Second Losses and Upsetville. These two tourist traps see plenty of action. I sped past them and headed directly for the main drag, Kick In Your Stomach Boulevard. How I arrived there at all needs a little backtracking.

In 1990, I saw a very interesting proposition at the Caesars Palace sportsbook. The prop was an over-under on Cecil Fielder hitting 50-1/2 home runs. Considering that he had 42 home runs at the time, and that there were 29 games to go, I figured there was a little value to betting the under. I walked around Caesars for a while pondering the bet, and left without making a wager.

Then I visited one of the all-around great guys of Las Vegas, the late Sonny Reizner, legendary race and sportsbook director at the Desert Inn. We got to talking as we usually do and I mentioned the Fielder proposition.

Sonny is known as the "king of the propositions," and rightfully so. He started the football contests in town and the Monday night parlay cards. Also, it was he who made the widely publicized betting line on "Who Shot J.R.?" There is probably no better source in the world to discuss a proposition bet than with Sonny Reizner.

We deliberated together for a long time, considering such factors as the weather (it would get colder in the latter part of the season and the air would be heavier); the pitchers (they were all now aware of Fielder); the pressure (the last time someone hit 50 or more homers was George Foster in 1977 in the National League and, in 1961, Maris and Mantle in the American League). Believe me, we analyzed this proposition inside and out!

Since the value was perceived to be there, I went back to Caesars and made my wager. Nothing really big, mind you, just a larger than average football play. The days passed and with each at-bat, the seasons' end was drawing closer. The odds didn't change dramatically in the context of at-bats versus home runs. In other words, the value of a further bet dictated itself.

Thus, I made another wager at -120 and a few days later, with no more home runs, I bet again at -130. Then, after a couple more days, I hit again at -130. After Fielder hit another homer, the odds went back to -120, but there was still a shade of value, so I plunged yet again.

A few more days passed and the odds became -160 on the under. Since there wasn't any value to be gotten at this price, I didn't bet. As any bettor with reasonable knowledge will tell you, the line will dictate your play.

Time was drawing the bet to its ultimate conclusion and Fielder now had 48 home runs with a week to go. Then he hit his 49th against Boston in his last turn at bat in the 8th inning. Only six games to go to close the season: three in Detroit against Minnesota, and three in New York against the Yankees. Statistically, Fielder was right on the number with a very slight advantage towards the under. The next five games yielded a lot of sweat on my part, but no home runs by Fielder. Nothing is more agonizing than not being able to watch your action on TV and being subjected to following it on the teletype machine located in the sportsbooks under the large screens.

The nation's sporting press grew larger and more intense with each passing day. When the last game finally arrived, the pressure on Fielder in New York was huge. For me to lose my bet, he would have to hit not one, but two home runs.

Friends and fellow bettors were already congratulating me. I knew better. After years of locking horns with the books, the only thing that makes sense is, paradoxically enough, what Yogi Berra said: "It ain't over 'til it's over." I told everyone to save the premature accolades until Thursday, the day after the final game.

The first two times up in this last game yielded no home runs. But on his third time at bat, Fielder smacked a homer just inside the left field foul pole for number 50. My heart did a topsy-turvy and I could find no place for my body. My cushion was gone. My bet was now reduced to an instantaneous moment and my mind was racing to that horrible place known as Bad Beat.

Finally, the 8th inning and Fielder's last at bat of the season. He already had his 50 homers and his team was comfortably ahead in a meaningless game. The odds in my favor were beyond good—in fact, they were great! The value in my wager was tantamount to buying a brand new Mercedes Benz for $1,000.

So why was I sweating? Why was my heart pumping blood so fast it affected my breathing? Mainly because I had seen this movie before, with an ending that tends to reinterpret itself over the years. Of course, he hit the 51st home run in his last at bat, crushing not only the ball, but me and many other bettors in a single stroke of his wand.

As with all bets, someone wins and someone loses. I had the right side, logically, statistically, and with an overabundance of value—especially going into the last game, let alone the last at bat.

So it goes. Bad Beat is a town that has claimed many souls. It's a city with no empathy, a place that should keep you from betting your house or car or your child's tuition. The only sure thing in Bad Beat is the probability of the unexpected.

Bad Beat's a town all gamblers have visited at one time or another. It's a really lousy place to spend any amount of time because it shakes your belief system and turns happiness into introspection. So my friends, watch out for that signpost up ahead. It's not the Twilight Zone—it's much stranger than that. It's a little berg called Bad Beat.

9

Betting College and Pro Basketball

by Lem Banker

The guy who usually tells you about the football taking crazy bounces is the guy who dropped it.

-- Lou Holtz

Winning isn't everything, but it beats anything that comes in second.

-- Paul "Bear" Bryant

Success is never final. Failure is never fatal. It's courage that counts.

-- Sam Rutigliano

Betting on basketball is different from betting on football and baseball. To succeed in basketball, you've got to be quick, and you have to have deep pockets. With more than 251 Division I college teams and 29 teams in the NBA, there are lots and lots of games, and the lines often don't go up until just a few hours before game time. It's not at all like football, where bettors have a week to chew things over before putting their money down.

A lot of money is bet on basketball, but with all the games—as many as 70 or 80 on a typical Saturday during the season—it's spread around more than in football or baseball. That's good for someone like me, who keeps his own numbers and is ready to exploit weaknesses in the lines when he sees them. The novice should be careful because basketball attracts a higher proportion of professional action than do the more "public" games of football and baseball.

A friend of mine in the brokerage business likes to say that betting on football and baseball is like buying stocks, which a lot of people follow, while betting on basketball is like being in commodities, a more specialized investment. "There are just two kinds of guys in commodities: the quick and the dead," he says. I think he's only partly kidding.

Basketball is similar to football in that its professional and college varieties don't have much in common from a betting standpoint. In fact, I think that differences between the pro and college games are greater in basketball than in the gridiron sport.

Season-to-season turnover of first-line personnel in college basketball can run from zero to 100 percent, but usually amounts to 30 or 40 percent a year. Talent turnover in real terms can be greater, because individuals are more important in basketball than in any other team sport. The loss of a dominant player has the potential to sharply change a team's fortunes.

On top of that, you have to realize that in college games, you're dealing with young players who can grow, mature, and improve a lot from one season to the next. And with all the summer camps and leagues they have these days, many do just that. Even a team with basically the same personnel can, and will, change from one season to the next.

There is some continuity in college basketball. Schools like North Carolina, Kentucky, and Duke, almost always have good teams, and a lot of others usually are no more than a half-step behind from year to year.

Since UCLA won those 10 NCAA championships in the 12 seasons from 1964 through 1975, only Duke has repeated as national champions in 1991-92. Also, we're talking about betting here, and even a small change in a team's overall strength can make a big difference in its success against the spreads.

The situation in the National Basketball Association is altogether different. As everybody knows, the key to success in the NBA is having a dominant center. All the top teams have them, and the big guys don't graduate or play out their eligibility like they do in college. The rest of the teams have to be bad enough to pick first in the draft in a year when a top center is coming out of college, or smart enough to get one in trade.

More important from a betting standpoint is that the pros play a long regular-season schedule of 82 games, plus a playoff schedule that every year seems to get longer and include more teams. An NBA game lasts 48 minutes and has a 24-second shot clock. The quick clock means that the players have to hustle up the floor to get their shots off.

Travel is tougher in professional basketball than in any other sport. Big league baseball has a 162-game regular season, but the baseball players play two-to-four-game sets in each city on the road, so at least they get to unpack.

In the NBA, it's one game in a town and out, battling crazy airline schedules in the worst weather of the year. It's big fellows crammed into tiny airline seats and beds built for average people. It's long games at high speeds against top opposition. Under those circumstances, it's difficult for players to do their best every night, which makes it a tough betting proposition for gamblers.

The bottom line is that I bet college and pro games very differently. College basketball, with its short schedules, limited travel, and eager young players, is a very defined game. I've never had a losing season in college basketball, even though I don't know the players on some teams from the parking-lot attendants at Caesars Palace. I've bet on NBA basketball in various ways over the years, and for three seasons I didn't bet at all. I was turned off by the drug scandals in the sport and the difficulty of finding a pattern to the point spread ups and downs that affect even the best of the pro teams.

I keep power ratings on the NBA, but the teams are like the new cars on a dealer's lot—every salesman knows their prices without having to look them up. This season, I've been betting the pros mainly on scheduling and psychology, and doing very well. I can't claim to have figured out the NBA on the basis of a half season's play, but I think I'm on the right track.

Like I said before, basketball is more of a professional game than either football or baseball, when it comes to gambling. The betting lines go up, get played fast, and come off, without the pounding (and distortion) by the public that you see in the other two major sports. You have to make judgments fast, and this takes practice. Don't rush into basketball without at least some preparation.

It's very important in basketball to shop the lines. When you bet games in volume like I do in the college game (I usually play between 60 and 80 games a week), a point here or a half-point there can make the difference between winning and losing financially. I wouldn't recommend betting on college basketball if you have only one betting outlet. At the very least, don't be shy about asking your bookie for a half-point here and there.

Don't go into basketball betting in a serious way without a big bankroll. There are lots of games, and you can disappear without a trace in no time flat.

10

THE SCOOP ON HOME COURT HOOPS

by Bryan Leonard
Professional Handicapper & Publisher, *Pigskin Report*
Football Newsletter

"We'll get 'em on our court." You'll hear professional and college athletes say things like this all year, be it in basketball's post or regular season. College basketball teams often play twice against conference opponents during the regular season, with each team splitting a game between their home court and the opponent's. Other times, teams can meet on a neutral court during tournament play and sometimes teams meet a third time in February and March during tourney time.

The site of a basketball game is extremely important, especially from a bettor's point of view. Spend some time going through the records—straight up and against the spread—of your favorite college and pro hoops' teams, and you'll be amazed at some of the differences.

Some teams will shoot the lights out at home, averaging 78 points per game. Yet, the same players can turn into certified masons on the road, averaging 59 points per game. It's not uncommon to find college basketball teams with an overall record of 11-10. But if you dig deeper into things, you may find that team is 10-1 straight up at home, and 1-9 on the road. Some teams aren't this extreme, but you'll find many that are. Clearly, something (actually, a combination of many things) is taking place. For serious sports bettors, it's important to identify these valuable wagering factors, apply meaning, and incorporate them into your handicapping. It's not only relegated to college hoops. Examine some of the home-road records of NBA teams over the years. One of the best examples is the 2000-1 Denver Nuggets.

The Nuggets were an average team with a 40-42 overall record. But something remarkable takes shape if you look closer: Denver had a winning spread record at home where they were 29-12 straight up. Yet on the road, a completely different team showed up, where the Nuggets were 11-30 straight up and 16-25 against the spread! All of a sudden, that's far from a near .500 team, isn't it? The Nuggets were one of the best teams in the NBA at home, and one of the worst on the road—both straight up and against the number!

Differences like this take place every basketball season, both in college and the pros. There are many reasons as to why this takes place. One is pride, which I hinted at in the beginning with the quote, "We'll get 'em on our court."

College basketball players at home have ten to fifteen thousand fans screaming behind them to play well, while booing the other team the entire game. In addition, professional basketball players know that the fans in the stands at home are paying their salaries, so it's likely that they will put forth a one-hundred percent effort to try and get a win for the home fans.

It doesn't make a lot of financial sense for players to give a lackadaisical effort and send the fans home unhappy, especially when fans are paying anywhere from $20-$200 for a ticket. That's like someone buying a brand new car, then having it fall apart on the drive home from the dealership. That automobile company would lose its fan base—and its business—fast.

When teams go on the road they are not always inclined to give 100 percent, especially weak teams. Psychologically players can be thinking, "We're not supposed to win here, so let's just get this over with and head home." This is why good coaches are so rare. Good ones have the capacity to motivate players to give it their all, whether they're at home or not.

Next time you watch a college or pro basketball game, watch what happens when a player at home makes a great block or dives out of bounds to save a loose ball. The fans will erupt at the player's effort. This all-out effort on the court can be contagious, and you'll often see that player run down the court, followed by teammates who will copy his all-out effort at both ends of the floor.

The crowd noise will grow even louder, which can result in momentum for the home team. This is why opposing coaches are so quick to call a time out when they see the home team and crowd going wild—they want to stem that momentum before the game gets away.

This also ties into emotion, which is a much larger part of college athletics than the pros. Simply put, a home team has more chances to get fired up and play hard in front of screaming home fans. At home, even bad teams can look like world champs for 48 minutes.

Another reason is confidence. Pro athletes are usually in their mid to late twenties or thirties, when confidence is most often developed. College athletes are aged 18-21 and are still learning the game and—just as important—they are still learning about confidence. And when a college road team gets behind by ten points, they can lose confidence, pack it in, and think, "Well, it's just not our night. We'll play better next time when we're at home."

Professional handicappers take careful note of rosters and identify which teams have an excess of youth and which teams have experience. You'll often find new coaches trying to build winning programs by getting their young players to learn to win at home, build confidence, and excite the fan base. Once they've developed that, the next step is to teach them how to win away from home. Sports bettors take note: This is a slow process that can take years to develop—and sometimes never does.

Smart handicappers pay close attention to this and it takes knowledge, experience and hours of study to begin to identify when these young teams might be beginning to blossom. From a bettor's perspective, for example, this offers opportunities "to play on" a young team at home and "go against them" when traveling.

Another reason for the home-road disparity is comfort. That is, players will practice at their own gym for a home game, where they know the layout of a building where the temperature and even lighting conditions are always the same.

If a guard shoots one-hundred jump shots at practice and gets in a groove, he knows the next day he'll be taking those same jump shots in the same building from the same place on the floor he just hit, say, 75 percent in practice.

But on the road, a player's comfort level can be very different. Players are taking bus rides, sleeping in airports or on planes, and even changing time zones. The comfort level is tweaked, and then they have to practice and play in unfamiliar surroundings, all of which contributes to the athletes not being at the same comfort level as when they're home.

With big-name college programs, history and mystique can also play a role. Visiting teams walking into the home arena of Duke, Indiana, North Carolina or Kentucky are often awed by the championship banners hanging overhead and the huge crowds rooting against them. Athletes won't admit that they're nervous about playing those schools, but deep in their minds they can be thinking, "We have no shot here. Let's just play this thing and get out of here. We'll get them later in the season—at our place!"

Sometimes schools have longer road trips than others, too. The Denver Pioneers happen to be in the Sun Belt conference (go figure), where they have to face mostly teams from the southeast, such as Arkansas State, Florida International, Arkansas Little Rock and Western Kentucky. Denver has to cross time zones to play its road games in conference play, just as their opponents have to when traveling to Denver. Many teams can look like world-beaters at home, and then go on the road the next game and look as sloppy as a kindergarten pick-up game. Sometimes a combination of factors can provide good go-against spots. And it's not just the big-name schools where this takes place, either. College basketball offers great opportunities for handicappers as there are so many games and extreme home-road disparities like this. You can find excellent betting edges in college hoops by looking at large conferences like the ACC, Big East and Pac 10, as well as smaller conferences such as the MAC, Sun Belt or WAC.

Also, when tournament time rolls around, you'll find teams playing on a neutral court. I examine the road records of both schools to see how each played away from home that season in an attempt to find edges. Some teams will be playing in their home state and may have more fans in the stands than their opponents, which creates a "near home court edge," which can sometimes mean making an adjustment in the number, though it's usually not as prominent as the normal home court edge.

So make sure you break down home-road stats in college hoops for teams and even individual players. If you see what you perceive to be a soft line, look carefully at how each team scores and defends at home and on the road. Just as miners and archeologists till the soil to unearth hidden gems, successful sports handicappers dig through stats and situations to find bad lines and winning plays.

11

THE HORSE PARLORS OF THE 1940s

by Tex Sheahan
Author, Gambling with the Best of 'Em!

Las Vegas has all kinds of gambling devices, such as dice, roulette, slot machines—and wedding chapels.
-- Anonymous

No horse can go as fast as the money you bet on him.
-- Anonymous

"All horse players die broke!" Sweeping statements like that always leave some room for exceptions to the rule, but any real chance of beating the ponies is probably comparable to finding the Holy Grail on an Easter egg hunt.

So perhaps I should rephrase that hypothesis to something like, "All inveterate and compulsive horse players usually die broke."

Back in the 1940's, in post war Chicago, I experienced the peak earnings of my gaming career and, in spite of being a lousy handicapper, I did manage to make a very good living on the horses.

But don't ask me for any hot tips because somewhere along the line, I hopped over the counter and wound up on the winning side—booking the bets instead of making them. That was about the only way for me to beat the nags.

In those days, the Windy City had a lot of "horse parlors" that hung sheets listing the entries and odds at as many as six tracks per day. Loud speakers updated the changing odds and jockey shifts, with full and accurate descriptions of all the races. They all paid the standard 30-12-6 ($62-$26-$24 for $2 on win, place and show bets).

Parlays were calculated on a 15-6-3 limit on each carry-over amount to the next horse, with a ceiling payoff of 100-1 odds. Exotic betting propositions, daily doubles, and quinellas paid off in the same way, at 100-1.

Another wagering option that was offered until sometime around World War II was the "house line," with a 20-8-4 limit. The attraction of these lower odds was that the bettor was guaranteed the posted line.

No matter what the after-race mutuels were, higher or lower prices, the players were assured of getting the house line payoff. Needless to say, a gambler who had something hot, or judged that he would be bet down, liked this action.

Beating the ponies was tough, with a strong percentage working for the house, but operating expenses were also high. It was a one-dimensional business, although some of these spots also ran poker at night, and maybe one low-limit blackjack table.

Bettors would go to any lengths to get their money down when the heat was on. And the bookies would continue to operate temporarily under the most adverse conditions.

I remember one horse parlor in particular—an enclosed, unheated area in the back of a plumbing shop. It was mid-winter in Chicago, with the temperature barely above zero. The wind was whistling through the big garage doors that served as a backwall, posing quite a problem for the four employees and some 40 or 50 customers. Wall sheets and racing forms were flapping around and tearing, and the close quarters were noisy from the sounds of patrons stamping their feet in an effort to keep warm.

But believe me, as the blackjack dealer, I had the toughest job of all. First, I had to deal while wearing a hat and overcoat. But my major problem was keeping the cards from blowing right off the table!

The loyalty (or addiction) of Chicago horse bettors was legendary. If the only "in action" book in town had been a wet, mucky 20 x 20 foot space in the bottom of a sewer, there would have been a full house every day in time for the daily double, with late arrivals hanging onto the access ladder.

Lots of colorful characters, right out of a Damon Runyan story, frequented these wagering establishments. For example, there was a public horse trainer named Max, who spent his evenings around a Chicago poker game I dealt. Public trainers usually handled horses for owners whose stable consisted of one or two horses that seldom won (called "vanity stables"), but carried their proud owner's silk.

Max's equine charges won about as often as leap year came around, but he still put out every nag he sent to the post as a "good thing." He must have had an affinity for losers— he was usually broke and always wore the same incredibly wrinkled suit, faded trench coat, and shoes with such run over heels they looked like ballet slippers.

But one night he came in flashing a bankroll that would have choked a couple of horses. He vowed that on his way out to the track, he was going to stop off at a men's store and buy a completely new wardrobe. However, that was one style show that never left the post!

We didn't see him for about a week, but when he finally came back, he was still wearing the same shabby clothes. Spreading his Racing Form on an empty poker table, Max told the guys about some plug he had entered in tomorrow's race: a maiden that was a lock!

Although no one had the nerve to ask about his new duds, he eventually related what happened. It seems he had gotten too late a start to drop off at the men's shop, and made it to the track just in time to catch the first race. In his own words, he explained, "I dunno how I could've missed seein' that horse in the first race... but there it was! Dressed To Kill its name wuz. I knew this was Lady Luck screamin' at me. So I keyed it with all 12 horses for twenty-buck doubles. Two-hundred and forty clams an' the dog never made a move!"

Stopping to light a cigar, he stared at the wall before resuming. "Anyway, it wuz all down hill after that... I musta' whammied every nag I bet on. Finally, this horse of mine wuz goin' in the last race, an' I only had four bucks left an' my ticket home. I bet two an' saved two, an' guess what? It won an' paid $38.60!"

Max was only one of the many plungers who made a lightning score and promptly parlayed it into a zero bankroll. You may still find a few of them around the Las Vegas sportsbooks today, where a lot of the retired railbirds and handicappers wind up.

Since there was no sports betting in those days, the sporting element were gamblers of single purpose—that of selecting winning horses and, in the process, slaughtering the bookie! And the bookmakers had to know the business from A to Z or they would be out of action.

Remember, there were no computers to handle the numbers for them, and no "offing" on the hot or "poison" horses, as they were called back then. They were on the board; they could be bet. Bookmakers were either professional or soon gone.

And kick this around: they had to pay for the rent, the wire service, salaries, utilities, scratch sheets, The Form for handicapping, hard cards, other supplies, and coffee for the customers—plus lots of sugar for John Law.

12

COMPUTERS AND THOROUGHBRED HANDICAPPING

by Rommy Faversham

Horse sense is what keeps horses from betting on what people will do.

-- Anonymous

If it weren't for betting on horses, some people wouldn't contribute to anything.

-- Anonymous

Some people are luckier with cards than with horses— because they can't shuffle the horses.

-- Anonymous

The emergence of computerized thoroughbred handicapping has received mixed reactions from horseplayers. On one hand, the whole idea behind "playing the ponies" is based on the premise that a racehorse's performance is not only reproducible, but predictable. Computers appear to be the perfect fit for compiling, processing and analyzing large amounts of information regarding the past performances of racehorses, thereby freeing the noble punter to engage in loftier pursuits. What could be better for the disciplined race enthusiast looking for that edge in both selection skills and money management? Naturally, there is another school of thought regarding computers in handicapping. This is the view held by the Fundamentalists, those who believe that the experienced human mind, with its ability to interpret the abstract, can and will out duel the demon silicon chip in any long-term handicapping battle.

The Fundamentalists will assert that they've never seen a single computer terminal in a paddock area checking for bandages or up at 5 am evaluating morning workouts. "We already know that horses don't read the *Daily Racing Form*," observed one veteran railbird recently. "What makes anyone think they'll read computer-generated speed ratings?"

The next vista of racetrack wisdom concerning computers would appear to be a fusion of the first two attitudes. The crucial feature is the appropriate perception of man and computer's respective strengths and weaknesses in outcome prediction. An illustration of this is found in a recent review by a leading independent consumer journal that rated three of four commercial racehorse handicapping software packages as "absolutely useless."

The general problem with these "pre-set" programs is that they base themselves on systematic methods that screen out information that is often necessary for successful handicapping. The horses chosen by these programs are almost "pre-ordained" by the inherent criteria employed and merely produce the same kind of selections over and over again. One commercially available program, for example, eliminates all first-time starters, claiming that "first timers can only beat a weak maiden field."

Obviously, a more complete method of analysis would take note of the horse's inexperience, while continuing to search for positive factors (good works, breeding, connections). The computer is limited by human-defined parameters and can only reaffirm the sometimes questionable handicapping notions of the software author. In James Quinn's excellent book, *High Tech Handicapping in the Information Age*, the author emphasizes the importance of wide and varied data acquisition. A broad spectrum of horseracing information can be viewed as a capital resource. Quinn goes on to divide handicapping analysis into five major branches: speed-pace, class-form, trip handicapping, pedigree, and body language. What we find is that each of these divisions differs in its ability to be studied with the aid of a computer.

Speed-Pace

Speed figures are easily generated by a computer and have become particularly important when analyzing spring events for older horses. These quantities are wholly numerical and are most conducive to the number-crunching capabilities of the PC. The most advanced programs (which I have reviewed) were able to make an automatic adjustment for track variant, as well as calculate expected time. The problem with speed figures is that they only reflect information easily appreciated in the *Daily Racing Form* and thus favor horses that are likely to be over bet. Perhaps the time has come to start enriching speed figures with additional, more esoteric information.

Class-Form

Class may be the single handicapping factor in which a computer with an extensive database may reveal the biggest treasures. The present class structure of thoroughbred racing is an inaccurate gauge of a horse's "true" class level. Computer programs have already been developed which seek to expose "hidden class" in a horse's previous competition by studying their subsequent performances.

Form handicapping, however, doesn't figure to benefit much from the Information Age. Computers may be able to derive a numerical value for form, but it is unlikely to offer much truly useful insight. Inside information from the stable itself is a much more powerful source of information regarding form. Although this type of information is infrequent, it doesn't require computer input.

Trip

Track bias data would be an interesting modification to speed figures in order to understand track conditions that favor or hinder early speed and-or certain rail positions. For now, however, the most useful electronic device for trip handicappers is not the personal computer but the television and VCR. Access to nightly replays of local races allows for a thorough analysis of strong performances and troubled trips. In addition, visual files on tape can be collected and easily recalled for review when a horse returns to the track.

Pedigree

One element of handicapping that cries out for computerization is the analysis of a horse's pedigree. The dosage profile has become a marvelous indicator of a young horse's likelihood to display early speed or to handle the classic distances. Computer acquisition of the updated rankings of sires and dams, as well as dosage profiles in all appropriate races, would definitely give the computer handicapper an edge.

If we do indeed ascribe to the theory that bloodlines are an integral component of a horse's racing potential, then it's silly not to explore the ways in which speed and stamina are expressed through each equine generation.

Body Language

The delicate art of understanding a horse's body language doesn't reckon to change much with the advent of computers and artificial intelligence. Even advances such as computerized analysis and reconstruction of a racehorse's gait do not figure to become available, or widely employed, by the handicapping public.

Making it with Money Management

Money management can be the horseplayer's final frontier. Handicappers can now take advantage of a wide assortment of money management programs in order to examine all of the factors that contribute to maximum profit. The Information Age has hammered home the concept that exotic betting (i.e. exact wagering) is more compatible with maximum gain at minimal risk. As multiple contenders are created by a broader system of analysis, the best betting opportunity becomes more of a "combination" type of risk.

A number of excellent hand-held computer systems are also available to identify profitable overlays on the tote by comparing possible mutuels on straight and-or exotic betting. From this brief discussion, it is evident that the question is not whether computers should be applied to the Sport of Kings, but rather, in what capacity? Quinn writes, "Handicappers should resolve to let computers perform the data processing, but complete the information processing and decision-making themselves."

Finally, the key to success in computer-aided handicapping is purpose. The Fundamentalists will benefit by freeing themselves of the relatively menial tasks of researching horse facts and figures and spending their time mulling over the bigger issues of outcome scenarios and value. They have lost no freedom of choice and can thank or blame no one for their fate.

In turn, the handicapper who already uses a computer must avoid making selections based purely on the limitations of a mechanical, systematic approach. He or she should use the computer to acquire and assimilate information and then use it to their advantage. With all of this in mind, let the good times roll.

13

EXOTIC BETS

A racehorse is an animal that can take several thousand people for a ride at the same time.

-- Anonymous

Every man has three secret wishes: to outsmart racehorses, women, and fish.

-- Anonymous

Most newspapers condemn gambling on the editorial page, and print racing tips on the sports page.

-- Anonymous

One of the truly fun events of the year happens on the first Saturday in May—the Kentucky Derby. Even if you have no interest in thoroughbred racing the rest of the year, for those fleet two minutes and a fraction, the country seems to hold its collective breath to watch the action at Churchill Downs.

Sportsbooks in Las Vegas have become very competitive, constantly challenging themselves to find new proposition wagers to test both your mind and your bankroll. The Kentucky Derby seems to be a "natural," an oasis of exotic betting opportunities.

For example, the following odds were posted for a past Derby:

Exotic Kentucky Derby Odds

Color of Kentucky Derby Winner	*Odds*
Chestnut	Even
Bay	4-1
Dark Bay-Brown	15-1
Gray	30-1
Roan	200-1

A female jockey will finish first:	150-1
A female jockey will finish second:	100-1
A female jockey will finish third:	75-1

There will be a Triple Crown winner: +2,000
There will not be a Triple Crown winner: -2,500

The winner will go wire-to-wire: +500
The winner will not go wire-to-wire: -700

The track condition for the Derby	*Odds*
Fast	1-7
Good	5-1
Muddy	10-1
Sloppy	20-1

The odds for which post position the winner would start from were also listed—all twenty of them.

For example, you could choose from post position one at 6-1; position four at 4-1; position 15 at 50-1; or, if you really wanted to gamble, you could have selected post position 16, 17 or 18 at 75-1.

What'll they think of next? Maybe what size shoes the winning jockey will wear? Or the owner's make of car? One thing you can be sure of: they'll think of some exotic new wager next year. You can bet on it!

14

DOSAGE AND THE KENTUCKY DERBY

by Rommy Faversham

One place where the professional gambler and the average-guy bettor part company is on being a fan. A pro gambler can't afford to be one.

-- Lem Banker

If it weren't for the dark days, we wouldn't know what it is to walk in the light.

-- Earl Campbell

A few of the also-rans hadn't even crossed the finish line in the 1991 Kentucky Derby when network television turned to veteran correspondent Jack Whitaker for his instant analysis of the race. "The long dosage streak is finally over!" he crowed. "Thank goodness!"

The barely completed classic seemed almost secondary to Whitaker as an ax of his was getting a good grinding. With two minutes of fine work, Strike the Gold became Dosage bashers' "poster child." His Dosage Index (D.I.) as calculated by Dr. Steven Roman was 9.00 and, therefore, well above the accepted ceiling of 4.00 for Derby winners. The chestnut's victory seemed vindication for those who saw only folly in attempting to predict a thoroughbred's distance potential through pedigree analysis.

A flurry of articles soon followed which sought to vilify Dosage as if it were witchcraft or much worse. *Racing Times* editor Kent Hollingsworth referred to the subject as a "sham" and a "canard." It mattered not that those who had become most vehement seemed to have the poorest understanding of the problem. Dosage, in fact, was never intended to be used as a handicapping tool. For almost a century, its study and practice was for the purpose of breeding a better racehorse through the balance of speed and stamina within one's pedigree. The Aga Khan created a racing dynasty in Europe after World War I by relying on its principles. Dosage would never become such a controversial issue until Dr. Roman found that his own updated version was seemingly well supported by the recent outcomes in the Kentucky Derby.

By the time Dr. Roman started producing positive return-on-investment (R.O.I.) studies with his Dosage index, the Pandora's Box had been opened. Dosage had become an angle for betting. It was now under the scrutiny of a whole new flock of critics.

When Strike the Gold won the 1991 Derby, it triggered a very unscientific response from Dr. Roman. The founder of "contemporary Dosage analysis" designated the colt's sire, Alydar, as a Classic chef-de-race, thus lowering his Derby winning son's D.I. below the acceptable limit of 4.00. This retroactive re-shaping of data, to make the numbers fit, not only looked self-serving, but was unsound as well. Most pedigree authorities view Alydar's influence on the breed as well to the left of pure classic (leaving Strike the Gold's D.I. well above 4.00). All the while, Dosage doubting vultures have been circling.

The misclassification of Alydar, combined with several other very questionable chef namings by Dr. Roman, led to the need for change in the direction of Dosage. An international panel of bloodlines analysts was recently formed to effectively deal with necessary amendments and updates to the system. Hopefully, order will be restored. As it stands, in the all-out search for the Kentucky Derby winner, the handicapper would be well advised to think in terms of simple pedigree analysis rather than rely on any dosage figure. Given the unique nature of the race, the punter should try to answer the following questions for each Derby starter:

1. Has the entrant's sire and broodmare sire been successful in producing offspring who could get the mile-and-a-quarter? Many of today's highly regarded stallions have not as yet demonstrated the ability to sire stakes winners at this distance.

2. Has the entrant's female family (the first, second and third dam) shown the ability to foal stakes winners at the mile-and-a-quarter distance or beyond? Most have not.

As the Derby approaches, articles in the *Daily Racing Form* and other thoroughbred periodicals should provide this information. Unlike Dosage, this data reflects the transmission of class and stamina within the exact lines from which the horse was bred.

Assuming the influence of pedigree on performance, there is a more direct relation between "what has happened before" and "what may happen again." The information will not be in the form of a tidy numerical value, but then that was always too much to ask.

With all of this said, never rely totally on any one source of information to handicap the big race. You must key on the more conventional indicators of class, speed and pace. As recent Derby history dictates, search for the properly bred longshot who's improving preps and careful handling signal surprise beneath the twin spires—maybe even a well-earned "dose of roses."

15

Betting Maidens

by Rommy Faversham
Horse Owner & Writer, *National Turf Magazines*

One day I bet on a horse so slow the jockey kept a diary of the trip.

-- Henny Youngman

The maiden race, whether claiming or straight, is a unique environment in the wide spectrum of horseracing's class levels. It is a one-way door that never opens for many, giving us the first glimpse of future greatness in a select few.

The relative appeal of the maiden race to the player varies from fascination to revulsion. It could, indeed, represent the "designated hitter's rule" of horseracing. Populations appear larger in the paddock area, as well as the concession stand, because of the more abstract nature of the undertaking.

Let's explore the various factors that must be addressed when properly analyzing the maiden encounter.

The Blood Will Tell

The most natural place to begin is with the horse's pedigree. The savvy horseplayer must be aware of those stallions which have demonstrated success in siring first time winners, the best reference being the current "Leading Juvenile Sires List," which may be found in select issues of *The Blood-Horse.*

The perennial leaders on this list are most often descendants of the brilliant chef-de-race, Phalaris, and the sons and grandsons of Northern Dancer, Raise a Native and Nasrullah. Keep an eye out for the following horses which have proven themselves as desirable sires of young runners: Alydar, Danzig, Vice Regent and his son, Deputy Minister; Mr. Prospector and sons Woodman and Gone West; Seattle Slew and his sons.

When a maiden race is run on the grass or a muddy surface, the appropriate sires' list should also be referred to and may be found in back issues of *The Blood-Horse* and *American Turf Monthly*. Also examine the maiden's female family. Very often, after a race has been run, the track announcer will point out that the young winner is a half-brother or sister to a famous stakes winner.

A final breeding matter is a maiden's month of foaling: information readily accessible in the *Daily Racing Form* and *The Racing Times*. A four-month gap in age within a field of two-year-olds can represent a significant difference in physical maturity. Late foals should be frowned upon unless they demonstrate an exceptional conformational development.

The Right Connections

The horse's connections are significant. It is a good sign when the breeder, known to sell portions of his produce, has retained ownership in today's young runner and also when the trainer is listed as one of the owners.

If the horse was bought at auction, it is useful to know the purchase price, which may be gleaned from the *American Racing Manual*. Further, some trainers just seem to excel with young horses, and handicappers are urged to keep some kind of record on them.

Jockeys are just as important as trainers. In a maiden race, which is usually run at spring distances, look for jockeys who are particularly adept at getting out of the gate well, which is characteristic of pilots who were schooled in Latin America. Many times, getting a good break and staying out of trouble is the only strategy a horse needs to make a winning debut.

No Experience Necessary?

In the maiden contest, there are typically very few lines in each runner's past performance and workouts take on an increased level of importance. Don't become hypnotized by the horse displaying a whole string of bullet works in the *Daily Racing Form*. Take note of trainers who always seem to get quick workouts from their young runners without any corresponding success in the afternoon. The best pattern is well-spaced works showing steady improvement.

Look for evidence of adequate gate (g) works. This will help to avoid the dreaded "broke slowly" trouble line. Also, look for the rarely awarded "b" for breezing. It's the best way a trackman can signify a particularly impressive work, regardless of the actual time.

The next major topic in maiden analysis is how to approach each entrant's prior racing experience. The listed class level is often an inaccurate gauge of a field's true collective ability. Many horse players are adept at assigning appropriate win probabilities within a given field, regardless of the rather simplistic class levels in use, i.e. statebreds and-or claiming price versus special weights.

Consequently, it is useful to observe the odds at which a horse previously went off. When other factors are theoretically equal, favor the horse that earlier went off at longer odds, for he was probably meeting a truly stronger field. Maidens who previously "outran their odds" can go on to win their next race without making a demonstrable drop in class. The reverse is also true.

Beware of the maiden who ran second or third as the favorite in its last race, since the horse could "unknowingly" be tackling a stronger group today. Many people wrongly assume that the *Daily Racing Form's* "Beaten Favorite Box" is a positive benchmark. What about the search for a "diamond in the rough," the winner of a maiden race at boxcar prices?

The best advice is to look for the horse that was previously competitive up until the head of the stretch before faltering badly. This group of longshots demonstrated reasonable early speed and got a valuable taste of battle, which often equips them to shock the crowd in a subsequent race. Consider body language. Look for good muscling, alert eyes and ears, and a glistening, dappled coat. Maidens with layoffs over 90 days should be considered in the same regard as a first-time starter. These types needed to return to the factory for repairs or schooling. Alterations in equipment and medication also need to be noted. The arguable race-enhancing effect of Lasix has a larger consequence in the maiden ranks than in events for older horses, primarily due to less lung scarring and thus greater pulmonary surface area in younger horses. The most underrated equipment change is adding blinkers.

The final issue is that of value. Maiden races are usually full fields and thus reward better prices for the winners. Despite this, the percentage of winning favorites in maiden contests on a national level is about 38 percent, well above the general average for all types of races. The crafty handicapper will note that 72 percent of all maiden winners are bet down from the morning line odds. Only join in when you deem the horse's chances and value are still worthy of a bet. While handicaps and glitzy stakes races are the figurehead of the sport, all thoroughbreds gotta start somewhere. And while claiming events for older horses may make up the backbone of racing, it is the maiden affair where it all begins. And remember: a long line of champions—including Affirmed, Dr. Fager and Kelso—all paid double-digit mutuels in their maiden voyage.

16

BETTING ON NASCAR

by Micah Roberts

Betting on NASCAR is a relatively new phenomenon in the bookmaking industry that has really taken off over the last seven years. Its rise in popularity coincides with NASCAR's rise in the television ratings. Only the NFL can consistently say their television ratings are better over that span. While the wagering action doesn't compare to the NFL's in Nevada, nor come close to the NBA or Major League Baseball, it is gaining ground on the NHL.

NASCAR has really established itself as a viable means of generating positive revenue for the books, while also presenting bettors with several angles to profit from. In the entire existence of Las Vegas sports books, there has never been a sport that just popped up out of the blue to become a major contributor in handle and the bottom line for books and also have a newly created attraction for the bettors.

All the major sports have always been there since the books first set up shop. The theories and booking strategies have always been set in place for those sports, passed down from one bookmaking generation to another, but with NASCAR wagering, it's the same yet very different from all the others. One thing is certain, bettors are catching on fast and as the seasons pass, they are getting sharper than ever with the sport.

Just like the other sports, the bookmaker has to look at all the past trends, guess who the public will play, and look at who's hot. The major difference between NASCAR and any other sports is the pre-staging sessions of qualifying and practices that offer valuable information to what drivers will do well on race day. However, the same theories apply to NASCAR wagering as it does with all other sports. Past trends are always extremely useful. We always hear trends associated with all the other major sports such as how the Denver Broncos have a great record at home against the AFC West opponents. Now we're hearing bettors discuss how Rusty Wallace's shorts track record is better than anyone's coming into a Martinsville race. When bettors start reeling off stats about a sport, you know it's arrived as a bettable sport.

There are generally two ways to bet on NASCAR: odds to win and match-ups-propositions. The odds to win are the most attractive to the general public and also the most profitable for the books. Only one driver can win the race and there is usually a theoretic hold of 35 to 40 percent of overall handle on the indexes.

For bettors allocating a bankroll of $20 to $200 a week on the car race, this is the option most take. They can win big with little, which is always attractive for any gambler in any gaming venture.

Some players do very well with the odds to win and allocate their money on several different levels. One of the more successful strategies I've seen has the bettor placing multiple odds to win wagers prior to qualifying. This bettor has already handicapped the race and has an eye on a few drivers based on past performances and also on how well the driver has done in like instances on the current year.

Like instances refer to similar runnings in the season. NASCAR has several tracks on the circuit that are similar and teams generally use the same set-ups at each of these like tracks. In 2002, Matt Kenseth had a great fourth place run in Atlanta on the fourth race of the season.

Three weeks later, Kenseth rolled into Texas and won. The tracks of Atlanta and Texas are very similar in banking, width, and configuration. The speeds run by the drivers are almost identical. The drivers who consistently do well on one will likely do the same on the other, particularly in this instance where similar tracks had races run in such a short span between the two.

To dig deeper into the race, the bettor can look at who has done well at the track in the last ten years. In the case of Texas in 2002, there were only five Winston Cup races run there. By looking at the past history, the records showed there were five drivers who did very well in all five races; Corpus Christi, TX natives Bobby and Terry Labonte, Dale Jarrett, Mark Martin, and Jeff Burton. That's five drivers from four different teams. The only teammates were Roush Racing's Martin and Burton, both past winners on the track, who also happen to be Kenseth's teammate.

The link between teammates is usually pretty strong. This wasn't the case two decades ago. Crew chiefs and drivers disliked the fact that a car owner felt the need to have more than one operation. No situation was more publicized than the initial two-car team of Rick Hendrick's in the mid 1980's when he had to ease tension between his own teams driven by Geoff Bodine and Tim Richmond.

They got jealous and constantly whined that one driver was getting better equipment than the other, so when a crew chief found something that worked, whether it was in the chassis set-up, shocks, or tire pressure at a particular track, they kept it to themselves and shared nothing with their teammate. These attitudes have changed over time and teams currently work very well together. Much of this has to do with the enormous amount of money that drivers and crew chiefs are paid. Single car teams are a thing of the past now, and the teams that withhold information from their teammates usually don't last too long.

For that 2002 Texas race, Kenseth opened 20-1. He had already won the second race of the season in Rockingham and later went on to finish the season with a series leading five wins.

At the Las Vegas Motor Speedway, we can see another example of dissecting past trends for success. Vegas has one of the flatter one and a half mile ovals on the circuit, comparable only to the sister two mile tracks in California and Michigan.

The Roush Racing team has been dialed in for each of the seven races held there through 2004. In five of the seven Cup races run there, Roush has come out on top. Martin won the inaugural race in 1998, followed by back-to-back wins by Burton. After taking a two-year break from their dominance at Vegas, Kenseth went on to win again for Roush Racing, back to back in 2003 and 2004.

After obtaining all the driver handicaps at the particular track, the bettors have a game plan prior to qualifying, and can weigh their options to win the most with the driver they like the most.

In the instance with Kenseth at Texas in 2002, a bettor may have only liked him as a third or fourth choice, laying two or three units with most of the money going to pre-race favorites Dale Earnhardt Jr. at 5-1, and Bobby Labonte at 10-1.

Junior finished second three weeks prior at Atlanta and was a past Texas winner. Labonte is the most successful active driver in Atlanta, despite having a 37th-place finish there three weeks prior, and has finished in the top 10 in four of the five Texas races run—not to mention the fact that he's from Texas. On some occasions, a homecoming can really get a driver focused, but ultimately, it still comes down to the car.

Now the bettor has the top three drivers with the most units laid out on them and he's looking for a couple of long shots that will pay off well at a unit play. "Texas" Terry Labonte, despite having a poor season, is still a past winner at Texas and has just as many top ten finishes as his brother. At 50-1, Texas Terry becomes a must play just because of his history there.

The next driver to look at is rookie Jimmie Johnson who is 30-1. Rookies rarely win races, but Johnson finished third three weeks prior in Atlanta and he's the teammate and protégé of Jeff Gordon, who also happens to own Johnson's car. Of the Johnson cars that Gordon started his co-ownership with Rick Hendrick, half were cars that Gordon had a tremendous amount of success with driving himself the prior year—most notably his terrific Charlotte runs in 2001.

Charlotte is also a track that is very similar to Atlanta and Texas. This information is important because we know Johnson should have a fast car for the track and the price definitely has value. Now it just rests on the rookie's ability to steer it.

Here's what tickets the bettor has now before qualifying:

> Earnhardt Jr.: 5-1 @ three units
> B Labonte: 10-1 @ three units
> Kenseth: 20-1 @ two units
> T Labonte: 50-1 @ one unit
> J Johnson: 30-1 @ one unit

Now the bettor is ready to take a look at the match-ups prior to qualifying. The match-ups and props are much different and have become a science to some. For the bookmaker, they can expect a theoretic hold of about four percent. Either Side A wins or Side B wins; there aren't 42 other opponents to go against like odds to win a race.

Players have done very well with the match-ups, and over the years the bookmaker has had to do some altering in an attempt to bring the edge back to the house and that four percent or better hold. Because of the unknown, many players don't have the confidence to play match-ups before qualifying or practices.

And if they don't follow the past trends, the stats say it doesn't matter. Over the last seven years, the driver that qualifies better in a match-up wins 60 percent of the time. It doesn't take a genius to figure out that by just following that formula alone, your chances are pretty good of winning in the long run. This particular bettor likes the sport of it, and while he bets following qualifying, he loves to find an early match-up that he believes is bad.

After compiling his list of drivers that should do well, he feels he has a better read on it than some of the books, and is willing to put his money down on it. He's looking for certain drivers, and he'll decide who he wagers on based on who they're matched up against.

Today he is looking for Junior, Kenseth, and B. Labonte, his top plays to win the race. He finds a match-up with Junior laying –120 against Dale Jarrett and passes because of Jarrett's strength at Texas. Bobby Labonte is a pick against Gordon and he passes there as well.

Then he finds Kenseth laying –130 against Steve Park and bets it for five units. Park has struggled up to this point in the season, but there is a hint of skepticism because Park is a teammate of Junior's. Nevertheless, he feels he's got the edge in this match-up based on his data.

Following the qualifying session, Bill Elliott is on the pole. His odds have been dropped from 25-1 all the way to 16-1. The value isn't really there with him anymore, considering he wasn't on the pre-qualifying list of drivers to look for.

When the bettor goes through all the channels of dissecting Elliott again, he sees that Elliott has five wins in Atlanta, but none since 1992, and he's driving the new Dodge for Ray Evernham, a new team with several question marks. A driver that does catch his eye is Ricky Rudd at 8-1. Rudd is driving the Yates Texaco Havoline Taurus and is a teammate of Dale Jarrett. Rudd qualifies third, and is fastest in the morning practice session.

He looks to play Rudd in a match-up with almost anybody and plays two units to win the race. The match-up he settles on is Rudd against Sterling Marlin who is leading the series in points and has already won two times in this young season. Marlin is also driving a new Dodge for Chip Ganassi, one of the most respected racing minds in Motor Sports.

But times tell the story. Marlin, despite all his great accomplishments on the season, qualifies twentieth and practices twenty-second quickest. Rudd has a huge edge based on the practices. Poor weather washed away the final two practice sessions, so those are the only times to use for this race.

In normal circumstances, the most telling sign of who will do well is the final practice session held on Saturday, prior to the race called "Happy Hour." Friday's early practice session is usually set up for the qualifying run, but on Saturday's they get set for race conditions. Whoever is fast in happy hour is likely to be fast in the race.

When the race is finally over, Kenseth wins the race, netting the bettor two units at 20-1, and also the match up for five units. Rudd finishes fourth, beating Marlin in the match-up who finishes seventh, for another five unit profit. The final profit tally for the race is 40 units.

The bettor played all the angles with research being the key factor and utilized all the post qualifying and practice information to find himself another nugget. As for the others, Jimmie Johnson runs an impressive sixth, Terry Labonte has his best run of the year up to that point with a tenth, Bobby Labonte finishes thirtieth, and Junior gets involved in an accident, finishing forty second.

It doesn't always work out that well, but the key is being consistent and following a personal formula. Utilize all the data out there. The Internet is the best source for this. Obviously, NASCAR.com is a great site for all past race results. But some of the other sites such as racingone.com and jayski.com have a great deal of useful information that'll keep any bettor in tune to what's going on in the world of NASCAR as it happens. As with any other sport, information is always the key.

17

BETTING ON GOLF

by Jeff Sherman

In recent years, golf wagering has become a staple in the mainstream of sports wagering. Unlike other sporting events, a wager on a golf event gives the bettor action over the course of four days. Golf wagering is accountable for roughly two to three percent of a sportsbook's handle, but has increasingly become available in more and more sportsbooks.

Considered one of the "fringe" sports along with NASCAR and the like, golf can help a sportsbook draw a customer base in the various sports on the wagering menu. In its early stages, the most common type of wager involving golf was in the odds to win market.

This can be found most frequently from sportsbook to sportsbook. There is often a wide variation in the prices on different golfers. Eventually, a few pioneers introduced matchups as a form of wagering.

This form is less prevalent from sportsbook to sportsbook as sophisticated bettors prefer to wager on matchups rather than odds to win. Now, the two represent the most common types of golf betting available, with propositions found most commonly during majors.

When Tiger Woods stepped on to the scene in 1996, golf wagering started to reach unprecedented levels. The sport had a true superstar that transcended the game. Before Tiger, the betting favorite would be priced in the 6-1 to 8-1 range.

With Tiger's consistent results and fan base, he would reach the point of being an odds on favorite! His odds would fluctuate based on his form in the even money to 5-2 range. This had been unheard of in an event composed of over 140 golfers.

Ever since the Tiger years began, the interest in wagering has increased tenfold. Not only are his odds short for a golfer, but when he was in an event everyone else's odds were dramatically higher. For instance, a group of golfers in the 40-1 range for an average tournament would often be priced in the 60-1 range when Tiger was the betting favorite. In essence, Tiger affected an event from a wagering standpoint just as he had from an economic standpoint for the tournament itself.

Another monumental event that brought golf wagering into the spotlight was the 2003 Colonial in which Annika Sorenstam became the first female to compete in a PGA Tour event in the modern era. There was the anticipation and uncertainty of how the best female golfer in the world would stack up against the men.

Novice bettors were introduced to golf wagering as a form of entertainment after the media craze had published the Las Vegas odds regarding Annika and her numerous propositions offered. Throngs of individuals who mostly wagered on football and basketball now got involved in golf for the first time. The two most popular propositions were her odds to make the cut and her over-under first round score.

The media brought so much attention to these that Annika herself even commented on the first round score set at 76 and a half at the Palms Resort Casino in Las Vegas by stating "Well, I can do better than that." And that she did, by posting an impressive 71. Following in Annika's footsteps, more ladies have attempted to display their skills in men's events and young phenom Michelle Wie narrowly missed the cut in the 2004 Sony Open in Hawaii and has as a goal of hers to one day play in the Masters. The most common way to bet a golf event is in the odds to win market. Most sportsbooks offer a list of a certain amount of golfers with a "field" option comprised of the other golfers not listed.

The number of golfers listed varies from sportsbook to sportsbook. Some offer a list 30 deep, some 50 deep, and sparingly one can find all golfers in the event with odds and no field option. There are dramatic differences week-to-week on golfers based mostly on their recent form.

The most noticeable variations come from whether or not Tiger Woods is involved in a tournament. If so, his odds will be low, while everyone else's will generally be higher than they would be if Tiger were not playing. The top golfers commonly start between 8-1 and 15-1, and longshots range from 150-1 to 200-1.

Other concurrent odds to win markets involve the offering of the next major, as well as odds to win the money list. Most sportsbooks that offer the odds on the money list close wagering at the start of the weekly tournament and it is then reopened Monday mornings.

Another option to wager on golf involves matchups. This is where one golfer is pitted against another, and it is up to the bettor to choose who will finish better in the tournament. The golfer who completes more holes wins the matchup. If both golfers play the same amount of holes, the golfer with the lower score wins the matchup. If two golfers are involved in a playoff, the one who wins the playoff wins the matchup.

The most common result comes from two golfers making the cut, and the one with the lower score wins. If one golfer makes the cut and his opponent misses the cut, the golfer who made the cut wins the matchup. If both golfers miss the cut, the one with the lower score wins the matchup. Golfers can be disqualified or withdraw and thus lose a matchup if their opponent continues to play one more hole than the unfortunate golfer.

157

Golf matchups from sportsbook to sportsbook can differ. As opposed to a game in which one knows the two teams involved, any two golfers can be matched up and a price given to the matchup. This allows for creativity and freedom by the bookmaker when making matchups. An example might be a matchup involving Tiger Woods against Ernie Els.

If Woods were a -180 favorite against Els, the bettor would wager $1.80 to make $1.00 if Woods wins the matchup. Conversely, if Els were a +160 underdog in the matchup, the bettor would wager $1.00 to make $1.60 if Els wins the matchup.

One sportsbook might offer Tiger against Els, while another sportsbook might offer Tiger against the likes of Vijay Singh or Phil Mickelson.

Some sportsbooks offer a 20-cent line, where the vigorish adds up to 20 cents in the favor of the house, as in the previous example. Some offer a 30-cent betting line. Some sportsbooks also offer daily matchups, in which the matchup is offered for the course of a round. The most common matchups remains those based on the entire tournament.

The other way to wager on golf involves propositions. These are commonly found during the four majors and a few other special events. Some propositions include wagering on the over-under winning score, golfers finishing positions, whether a golfer will make-miss the cut, and will there be a playoff.

For instance, Tiger Woods's finishing position might be offered at over-under 4.5 with an associated price. This means one can wager on whether Tiger will finish in first through fourth place (including ties), or fifth or higher. The most propositions are offered for the Masters, the most heavily wagered tournament of the year.

The internet has become a good source to check golf odds. There are websites all over the world that have information for wagering on golf. Golfodds.com is a new addition that offers Las Vegas golf odds in addition to links to golf websites pertinent for golf wagering. Odds on a weekly tournament are posted each Monday and information is updated daily.

CHAPTER
5
INFORMATION YOU NEED TO WIN

1

INFORMATION

If you bet on football (doesn't everybody?!), a friend or a bartender or someone you work with will come up to you with "inside information" on next weekend's game. "It can't lose," your well intended source will tell you.

But most of the time they will be passing along old news, not inside information. What is inside information, anyway? How does it affect the betting line? Where does it come from? Is it opinion or fact? I posed those and many more questions to the wisest of football betting wise guys, sparing no effort in tracking down many of the true legends in sports wagering. To list all of their accomplishments would take up this entire book, so I'll be brief.

Here is the expert panel (alphabetically):

Lem Banker: Las Vegas' most successful sports bettor and co-author of Lem Banker's *Book of Sports Betting*.

Mike Lee: Winner of the prestigious Las Vegas Hilton Superbook Football Contest. Winner of the Castaway's Ultimate Challenge. Publisher and chief handicapper of *The Moneymaker*.

The late **Sonny Reizner**: Co-author of *Sports Betting With Sonny Reizner*, much sought-after speaker and lecturer. Former Race and Sportsbook director at the Desert Inn Hotel in Las Vegas, Nevada.

Michael "Roxy" Roxborough: Former President of Las Vegas Sports Consultants, Inc. Plain and simple, Roxy made the line we all bet into. Author of *Race and Sportsbook Management*, featured on CNN's "Crossfire," CBS's "48 Hours" and in *Newsweek*.

Chuck Sippl: Senior editor of *The Gold Sheet*, considered the Bible of football bettors. In the words of *Gold Sheet* publisher, the late Mort Olshan, Chuck is "an astute observer of the handicapping scene and as close to a perfectionist as there is in the business."

Although many people are successful sports bettors, these men are that and much more. They are respected for doing their work honestly. You'll never hear any of them talking about a "lock" game, because they simply don't exist. The most any qualified bettor wants is value—getting your money's worth.

Lem Banker has made a career out of getting value. He shops lines in Vegas sportsbooks with an almost super-human tenacity. In Las Vegas, sportsbooks offer different pointspreads. Most are the same, but during the course of the day, the line moves up and down according to that particular sportsbook's incoming wagers. Watching Lem work, with a phone in each ear and the automatic dialer tuned into his many casino accounts, is like watching a master paint. Lem isn't gambling per se; he is intelligently moving money and getting the best of a tough situation.

Value: to many, just another word. To Lem, it's a way of life. "There's an old saying that if you want to be a millionaire, make book inside the jockey's room," Lem says. "I get inside information all the time; sometimes it's good, but most of the time the bookmakers and pricemakers know about it and the price becomes inflated. What happens is the bettor pays retail price instead of wholesale. If you get original information when it's still fresh, you have a good shot at winning. Unfortunately, most people are followers and in most cases, they will lose."

Adds Banker: "Most people mean well when they give you a tip. Almost every week you'll hear this or that. I like to bet on bad teams when I'm getting value and against good teams when they're overpriced. I go by statistics because there is no hometown bias. But you have to be sharp in looking at stats because, in many cases, they can be misleading. Many teams that lose have more yards passing simply because they are behind in the score and are trying to catch up. Also, the team that's ahead gives up short passes in the middle of the field to eat up the clock.

"Yards rushing is a good indicator of how the game is played." So what does a legendary wise guy sports bettor read to enhance his knowledge? Banker says he reads both Las Vegas daily newspapers, plus *The Los Angeles Times, The Gold Sheet, The Moneymaker* and *The Sports Reporter.*

"Most rumors simply don't stand up," points out Banker. "The best advice I could give is, 'Let the buyer beware.' If a number goes from six to seven and a half, I like to go against public opinion and take more than a touchdown." At times, inside information can be the light at the end of the tunnel for the sports bettor. Unfortunately, more often than not, it's an oncoming train!

The late Sonny Reizner has seen many a sports bettor come to Las Vegas with a swagger and a bankroll to match. Having conquered their hometown, they think they're ready for the major leagues—the final assault on untold riches and a life of easy money.

Almost every one of these guys busts out in less than a season as the result of their own laziness, sloppiness or lack of money management skills. As the song goes, "When you plant ice, you're gonna harvest wind."

I asked Reizner how he deals with inside information. "There are two kinds," Sonny says. "Some information has to be respected, but most of it is pseudo-inside information, and that is nothing more than malarkey."

Reizner put out the line on "Who Shot J.R.?" many years ago when betting on non-sporting events was still legal. He was also the father of the legendary football handicapping contests at the long-gone-but-not-forgotten "Hole In The Wall" book at the now-defunct Castaways, which used to stand on the section of the Strip now occupied by The Mirage.

"After years of being involved in sports betting, you know that certain people just like to spread rumors," reports Reizner. "Also, the longer you gamble, the more you last, the better you become at handicapping the games and also qualifying the information you receive. Information is extremely important, but you shouldn't accept it or discard it without looking into it. You must take the time to check out the rumors. You *must* investigate."

Handicapping is much like life in general. As Reizner says, "You have to understand the difference between fact and opinion. It can be a costly learning experience."

So how is the line affected by rumor? What information does the linemaker use and where does he obtain it? Michael "Roxy" Roxborough was the man that created the Las Vegas line for many years. In his former position as a linemaker, his input was a critical component of the sports wagering business. Roxy used to bet, but because of an obvious conflict of interest, he didn't wager while he was setting the line.

He did, after all, have more action on a daily basis than anyone in the world. He touched the lives of people he doesn't even know. Roxy was the man who creates half-point wins and losses. He was the needle from which the adrenaline flows.

"We were always statistics oriented. I didn't think the emotional highs and lows were an overriding factor in the games. We go by the numbers," says Roxborough. "Injuries sometimes have a tendency to get overrated. You have to know how valuable the person is and how valuable his replacement is and then make an assessment from there."

Agreeing with Roxborough, Lem Banker recalled the sixth game of the 1982 NBA finals: "Kareem Abdul-Jabbar sprained an ankle in the fifth game and didn't make the road trip to Philadelphia. Magic Johnson fills in at center. It looks like a 'can't miss' for Philly. Of course, Magic plays great and the Lakers win the championship. No one can make a living off inside information. Some bettors bet the other way after the line is adjusted because they think the line is over-adjusted," declares Roxborough.

What information does Roxy depend on? "We have five different wire services: Sports Network, Sports Ticker, U.S.A. Sportswire, Associated Press and Computer Sportsworld," Roxy explained. "Newspapers are better for perspective, but the late-breaking news is on the wire."

Mike Lee is one of the few handicappers whom everyone respects. He has earned this respect by winning prestigious handicapping tournaments and, more importantly to the Vegas bettor, by his work ethic and objectivity.

"True inside information is kept among a certain group of elite insiders; it's something the public doesn't know about. I don't put a great deal of emphasis on it," says Lee. Work, work and more work is his approach to handicapping.

"You must assimilate all the information as best you can," he advises. "Devour all the data you can get your hands on. Inside information, for most people, is the easy way out. It's for folks looking to make quick, easy bucks."

Lee continues, "In football, the best player does not mean more than three points to the line. I base my selections on a degree of variance from the line I make. I take stats and use certain formulas to put the data in context and find the overlays that I need."

He recalls a story of inside information that still brings a smile to his face. "A long time ago I had a very successful month in college basketball where I won 66 games and lost only 32. I found out later from a friend who was following all of my selections that, in many of those games, my selections came on the injured side. He couldn't believe it. Ignorance is bliss indeed!"

A bit of inside advice from Mike Lee: "I wouldn't switch from team A to team B based on only one source of information."

The Gold Sheet has been in business since 1957. Everyone who bets football seriously refers to it. Packed with statistics, the test of time has shown that it can be trusted. Chuck Sippl, its senior editor is right in the center of this information factory. What is inside information to Sippl?

"Something the public would not be aware of: injuries, the team's mood, how they're going to approach the game. Is there going to be a special effort? Or are they looking ahead? These are some of the things we look at."

"Information is power. The more information at your disposal, the better your chances of success," stresses Sippl. "You're only as good as your information. Some information can be misleading; that is, you can get biased information if a person is too close to a team and if that person allows his personal feelings to mislead him as to the strengths and weakness of that team. We search for solid information, not opinion," he adds. "After we get the information, then the staff of *The Gold Sheet* forms an opinion of what's going to happen in the game. Of course, we check out all information."

Sippl says his scouts phone in injury reports and the status of the injured player's backup. "Ten to twenty percent of the time, someone knows someone who knows something. Most of the time, bias enters into it. Trainers and coaches are generally poor handicappers," he adds.

"Remember years ago when Thurman Thomas was out for a couple of games for Oklahoma State? The word was out to bet against OSU. The only trouble was that his backup was Barry Sanders," Sippl smiled.

"The point spread on a game will move more rapidly on an unsubstantiated rumor than it will for a bona fide injury that will affect a team's play. This has happened over and over again," cautions Sippl. "If a bettor can't substantiate a rumor, he might be best served to stay away from that particular game."

The next time—and it will more than likely happen before this football season ends—someone comes up to you and offers you friendly advice about "inside information," do yourself and your bankroll a favor: check it out first. There are no easy answers to handicapping questions.

2

MISINFORMATION

If you hang around a casino or sportsbook long enough, you'll hear just about everything. The other day, I was in a Vegas Strip hotel sportsbook and there were three guys in their mid-fifties talking loudly in the seats right behind me. One of them was talking excitedly and the word 'system' kept finding its way into the conversation.

Since 'system' is such a buzzword, my ears perked up and I positioned myself so that I could hear everything. I'm glad I didn't miss what was to follow because, if I hadn't heard it with my own ears, I would have had a very difficult time believing it.

It was a little before seven p.m. and most of the early games were in the eighth or ninth inning. The Blue Jays were playing the White Sox with the score tied. One guy said, "Who do you like in the Reds-Dodgers game?" It was going to start in about half-an-hour. Mr. Know-It-All replied, with the utmost confidence, "If the Blue Jays win, take the Reds. If the White Sox win, take the Dodgers. I've got a system on TV games. It's worked about 90 percent of the time."

This is a direct quote, folks! I couldn't understand how an adult sports bettor could possibly come to these conclusions. What's worse is that the other two guys accepted his opinion as gospel truth.

Never underestimate the gullibility of people who wager.

This leads me into a subject that should be considered by everyone who bets on sports: what is good information? Obviously, a few good sources are *USA Today*, with all of its in-depth charts and status reports, and *The Gold Sheet* is a singular must for football bettors because of its reliable statistics and game-by-game analysis. Television and radio provide up-to-the-minute reports on various teams and games that might be important to your betting interests.

Also, there are many books and magazines that offer an overview of the season and each team's strengths and weaknesses. And, of course, the internet with all of the websites that provide critical and up-to-the-minute information.

But let's get back to what I started writing about in the first place: misinformation. People who swear by systems that, in most cases, don't have any factual foundation, are similar to snake oil salesmen. On the surface, you want to believe them, but if experience teaches us anything, it is to beware of the charlatans who come to us disguised as friends and touts. These people have cost the betting public more money than the stock market.

The 10-star lock, the 100-star lock and the soon-to-be-released infinity lock are misnomers. You see, folks, there are no locks in sports betting. That's why there's a point spread! The point spread is the great equalizer. The notion that someone holds the key to the great gate of sports betting knowledge is at once implausible and insulting to your intelligence.

The best and most honest handicappers are extremely happy to win 60 percent of their games. For anyone slow in math, that's winning six and losing four in ten betting situations. Now let's use some common sense: if the best of the best are very happy to accomplish 60 percent, what does that do to the lock system tout's theory? Obviously, it shoots them down to the ground where they deserve to be buried. A word to the wise: don't get buried with them.

3

THE MYTH OF THE LOCK

Gambling is pretty much like liquor; you can make it illegal, but you can't make it unpopular.

-- Anonymous

Experience is a hard teacher because she gives the test first, the lesson afterwards.

-- Vernon Sanders Law

Shallow men believe in luck. Strong men believe in cause and effect.

-- Ralph Waldo Emerson

Just when you think you've got it made is when you'd better start looking over your shoulder. That's the way it is in real life and also in gambling. First of all, I'll state the obvious: there is no sure thing! At times, you might get the best of a given situation and, in a safe and sane world, you would always win.

Many people who should know better—and sometimes do know better—insist that a certain wager is a sure thing or, as they put it, a lock. During football season, many people who never bet during the rest of the year get serious about pointspreads and totals.

Do yourself a favor this coming season: do not take anyone seriously who says a game is a lock!

This person is either an idiot who has no comprehension of handicapping or gambling in general, or a charlatan who is going to rip you off and steal your money, sooner or later. Certain games appear to give the bettor an advantage and, in some cases, the reasoning holds true. Just because someone tells you about a certain game and all their insights become reality doesn't mean the game was a lock, even if they told you it was prior to the game. All it was, in effect, was good handicapping.

Many so-called scamdicappers will use any devious means to take advantage of squares. Giving out both sides of a game is an obvious way to keep half the people satisfied and coming back for more.

As with everything in life, there is good and there is bad. Unfortunately, in sports wagering there are more people trying to take advantage of the naive sports bettor than there are honest and hard-working handicappers trying to earn a living by helping the bettor. Most people don't have either the time or the inclination to do their own handicapping, so they look for outside help. One of the key mistakes these people make is to telephone the person with the biggest advertisement.

If you wager, you probably travel in a crowd that also bets. Ask your friends what they do. If they call a 900-number, do they believe they are getting their money's worth?

I personally know many honorable people who are legitimate handicappers. They do an honest job and work long hours to come to their conclusions. In my opinion, they are the exceptions to the rule. Consider yourself warned by someone who has nothing to gain by telling you the truth—except your respect.

HANDICAPPING
WITH COMPUTERS

A terrible accident happened to me on the way to the racetrack. I got there safely.

-- Henny Youngman

I never make excuses. You either ride a horse good or you ride him bad.

-- Bill Hartack

Handicappers are always looking for an edge. In most cases, they won't find it, but will be happy enough to settle for value. Handicappers take many different roads to discover facts and figures in order to determine how much one team is better than another.

Newspapers such as *USA Today* have an excellent sports page filled with facts and breakdowns and schedules that fulfill many of the handicapper's obvious needs. If you wager on football, *The Gold Sheet*, a weekly newsletter, is a must. Also, local newspapers feature stories and facts about their teams that could make the difference between winning and losing.

Those of us who live in Las Vegas, the gambling capital of the world, are very fortunate. We can shop lines and get an extra point here and there. That little difference can make a huge difference in our bankrolls over the course of a season.

Many handicappers have broken through the pencil and paper barrier and have forged forward to the instant access world of computers. From this vantage point, I see and hear diverse things pertaining to the world of handicapping. Regarding computers, the most often quoted phrase I hear is "faster and easier," the same reason our forefathers switched from a horse and buggy to an automobile, faster, easier and much more efficient.

In an age when knowledge is king, the faster you receive information and put it to use, the longer you'll stay on top. The better and more accurate the information, the more chance you'll have to beat the odds.

Because there are so many variables in the makeup of a line and whether you should bet into it, a computer is not just a way to get ahead of the game, but more of a method for keeping up with it.

Weather conditions during a football or baseball game can make a tremendous difference in your selections, especially in your over-under plays.

Totals in games at Wrigley Field can vary as much as five runs depending on the direction in which the wind is blowing! Up-to-the-minute line-up changes can and should affect your action, as does the mountain of information about the game itself.

How about the wonderful wacky world of horseracing? I don't know how anybody can physically and mentally keep up with all the horses at all the tracks and still find time to eat and sleep. Wouldn't it be easier to press a couple of buttons and get instant information on thousands of horses and their past performances? Their times at different distances, which fields they've beaten, where they've run—all at your fingertips?

That's what the world of computers has to offer. Consider this: the casinos have them. Doesn't that tell you something important?

5

INTEGRITY A

From the *Daily Racing Form*, March 15, 1992

by David Scott
Sports Columnist, *Daily Racing Form*

The answers to three questions will determine your success or failure: Can people trust me to do my best? Am I committed to the task at hand? Do I care about other people and show it? If the answers to these questions are yes, there is no way you can fail.

-- Lou Holtz

This is a story of checks, lies and audiotape. It's also a tale of greed, deceit and betrayal, with enough charges and recriminations to satisfy a Hollywood tabloid show producer. Here's the script:

Up until March 4, 1992, Larry Grossman worked for KVEG radio, hosting a daily talk show in the 3-5 p.m. slot called *You Can Bet On It!*

This being Las Vegas, where gaming not only is legal but revered, Grossman's studio guests often included casino bookmakers, professional gamblers, handicappers and touts. While these may be pejorative terms elsewhere, being a bookmaker, gambler, handicapper or tout in Nevada is a lawful, if not honored, profession.

In Grossman's two and a half years with the station, he had presented a variety of guests, including authors Jimmy Breslin, Peter Gollenbock, Burt Sugar and Tom Brohamer, as well as gaming industry gurus such as Michael "Roxy"

Roxborough, president of Las Vegas Sports Consultants and the nation's leading oddsmaker, *Gold Sheet* founder and publisher Mort Olshan, and Sonny Reizner, race and sportsbook director of the Rio and a legend and pioneer in the field. "One of the main purposes of the show was to present handicappers who would talk about upcoming games in an honest and truthful way that would give the player a chance to understand sports betting," Grossman said.

Grossman says his troubles with KVEG started when, despite his protests, an ad from handicapper B.T. Sisson began to run on his show. "My objection to B.T. Sisson was that he made ridiculous claims. He said he won 102 out of 104 weeks in baseball and that he was winning in basketball at a 68 percent rate. I knew that was patently absurd and I objected to his advertising on the radio station."

Roxborough has heard it all before. "If every sports service won at the rate they claimed, there wouldn't be a bookmaker left standing in the Western world," he said.

Sisson, 54, a Virginian who says he owned a trucking company in Charlotte, North Carolina, before coming to Las Vegas, admits he handed over a check for $1,900 to KVEG for three weeks worth of advertising on the station.

Grossman says Vince Lupo, the station's sales manager, and Jerry Kutner, the owner, began to pressure him to put Sisson on his show, citing Sisson's advertising dollars as the rationale. Lupo and Kutner deny they pressured Grossman.

"It's bad enough you're playing the ad on my show," Grossman says he told Lupo and Kutner, "but I won't perpetuate this fraud by having Sisson on my program."

Grossman said he enlisted the aid of Jack Stewart, the owner of Sports Watch, a Las Vegas monitoring service, to help convince Lupo that Sisson's claims were untrue. Stewart says he told Lupo as much, but Lupo says he has "no recollection" of Stewart saying anything derogatory about Sisson.

Grossman says he finally relented and agreed to put Sisson on the air, only after receiving assurances from both Kutner and Lupo that he could ask Sisson "hard questions." Kutner says he never gave such an assurance, but Lupo did. Lupo says he "can't recall" providing such an assurance.

On March 3, 1992, Sisson went on *You Can Bet On It*. Grossman and Sisson listened to Sisson's radio commercial:

"This is B.T. of B.T. Sports. My proven, untouched and unblemished record in basketball and baseball is without equal. In the last two years, my validated record in basketball is 68 percent and in baseball, I've accumulated an astounding 102 winning weeks out of 104. Not too shabby, babe."

Grossman wanted to know how Sisson could have 102 out of 104 winning weeks in baseball over the last two years.

"The ad is misleading in that extent," admitted Sisson. "It was supposed to be 102 out of 104 betting weeks, over the years. What that really means is that if a bettor follows my picks, and we tell a person how much to bet on what teams, he will come out a winner at the end of the week."

Challenged by Grossman on his contention that he'd selected 68 percent winners in basketball, Sisson, who provides his selections over a 900 number, said he based his claims on a dollar figure, not wins and losses.

Furthermore, he said, he'd been monitored by—get this—Jack Stewart of Sports Watch, who he said was "very honest."

Then Grossman took a telephone call from (and isn't this delicious?) Jack Stewart. Stewart said Sisson was the handicapping leader in baseball during the first half of the season, but that his record after the All Star break was 106-133. Sisson said that during the second half of the season he'd been working as a car salesman—you can't make this stuff up, folks—and hadn't devoted the necessary time to handicapping. Throughout the show, Grossman's questions, if pointed, were asked in a polite manner. Sisson, for his part, never seemed shaken.

The next day, Grossman was fired. "We made a programming change," Kutner contended. "It's just coincidence he was fired after the show."

"That's a lie," said Grossman. "Kutner told me I was fired because of the way I treated a major advertiser."

Sisson feels he was "set up" by Grossman and called Stewart's comments "a bunch of lies." He acknowledges that the fallout from the show has damaged his business. "One fella was going to invest 50 grand, but after he heard the show, he said to forget it."

Stewart called Sisson's handicapping claims "out-and-out lies," categorizing his radio ads as "totally false."

"My show had credibility," said Grossman, "and I wasn't going to let people listen to Sisson's garbage without me challenging it. You can only lose your integrity once, and then it is gone forever. If I had it to do all over again, I would."

You can bet on it.

6

INTEGRITY B

Most of the best people I have ever had the pleasure to associate with have been involved in gambling in one way or another. The honesty and integrity these men and women exhibit on a daily basis, both professionally and personally, would embarrass their civilian counterparts.

By its very nature, gambling requires a certain degree of trust. Decisions involving large amounts of money are instantaneous. All interested parties need to resolve matters immediately and permanently before the next hand can be dealt. True, there are occasional arguments about the interpretation of the rules. But the gambling world is far removed from the "real" world, where a contract is only as good as your lawyer's connections. In gambling, the same rules apply to everybody equally.

People on both sides of the counter are generally fair and live by a code of conduct that they all understand and abide by. If you say, "I want a $30 six and eight," and the dealer replies, "Bet," you have action. Plain and simple, no sales receipt. Your word is your bond.

That's the way it used to be in all sectors of society. A person was expected to tell the truth, and usually did. But in today's fast paced civilization, with so many people playing fast and loose with the rules and their words and actions, the credibility that once was taken for granted must now be proved.

Las Vegas has always been a tough town. Many people have come here with visions of grandeur. Success doesn't come easy here or anywhere else. It has to be earned. Almost everything of value has to be earned. You don't get to be an

Olympic athlete or a world champion of poker by luck. You work at it and take your lumps. Sometimes you go broke, but you learn from your experiences. If you have the talent and the heart, you'll rise above the mediocre.

Someone once said, "The beauty isn't in the achievement, the beauty is in the struggle." At birth, we are all blessed with something no one else can have or take away from us. We can only lose it or foolishly give it away. We should value it, cherish it, and allow it to grow. That "something" is integrity.

We will all be tested in our lifetimes, sometimes obviously, other times subtly. But the moment will come when someone will try to buy our integrity, or steal it, or somehow tarnish it. When your moment arrives, hold on and don't let go. You can sell it only once, and even if you are the only person who knows it's gone, it's gone forever.

Recently, I faced a situation that I knew was wrong. I was called on to betray people I had never met, but respected all the same. I lost my job—a job I loved more than anything I had ever done in my entire life.

The truth is, there was no decision to be made. What you're made of is more important and more meaningful than what you do. My refusal to knowingly dupe my radio audience, as my previous radio station did, led directly to my firing.

We in the media have a certain moral obligation to tell the truth and to protect the public from the abuses that are thrust upon them. Certainly, we should never help to perpetuate a lie that could cost our audience, just to satisfy our own needs.

There are those who consider my stand heroic. Not so. I only did what I would expect others in the same situation to do. There is right and there is wrong. The gray area in between is much smaller than many people would care to admit.

When people make false claims and others in positions of power perpetuate their lies to dupe the public out of their hard earned money, it's hard to figure who is more the villain: the perpetrator or the propitiator.

We can't always ask the government to protect us from the enemy within. If a deal seems too good, listen to the voice inside of yourself and just say no.

The gambling community of Las Vegas in particular, and of the world in general, needs to police itself and not let the few who are not gamblers at heart put a stain on people's perceptions of us. The gambling industry in Nevada is legal, and is the major contributor to our way of life here in Las Vegas.

Let's not allow the quick-buck artists who think flim-flam is a routine business exchange get away with ruining what has taken years of hard work and honest effort to build. Let's not give them a chance to destroy the novice's perception of what gamblers and handicappers are truly about.

Gambling is risk. You can win and you can lose. But let the law of averages determine what will happen—not somebody who has no remorse in perpetuating outrageous claims, or someone who would take money from the Devil himself just to pay the electric bill.

CHAPTER

6

MONEY MANAGEMENT

1

The Dogs Were Barking

If you never learn another thing from this writer, please commit this fact to memory: Bet more when winning and less when losing. This is a basic tenet of getting full value for your gaming dollar. The importance of this money management strategy and its' effects on your bankroll were never more dramatic than what happened in the 1990 NCAA basketball tournament.

Eight games were played on a Sunday in that tourney and, believe it or not, all eight underdogs covered the pointspread. An incredible 8 for 8! This was either good news or bad news, depending on how you wagered. If you bet all the underdogs, did you take full advantage of a once-in-a-lifetime situation? Or, if you bet all the favorites, did you get destroyed?

I was comfortably seated in my favorite sportsbook on that historic day and spoke with several bettors who were either deliriously happy or terribly depressed. The happy people were obviously easy to talk with and eager to give details on every game they won.

I didn't want to get too involved in why they picked the underdogs, but rather, what was their betting strategy? It's one thing to pick a winner and quite another to take advantage of it monetarily, which is, of course, the essence of gambling.

Unfortunately, most of the underdog bettors I spoke with were very satisfied to have won and didn't want to tempt fate by increasing their wagers. Many of these folks actually decreased the size of their bets as the day wore on—hence, they won only a fraction of what they could have.

Perhaps even more interesting is what happened to the "favorite" bettors. After losing game after game, the last bet of the day was coming up. Gamblers traditionally know this game as the "get out" game because it's their last chance to "get out alive," so to speak, if they're losing. During football season, the Monday night contest is the "get out" game—and it can be a crusher!

Arizona, one of the best basketball teams in the country that year and a pre-tournament favorite to win the whole enchilada, was chosen over Alabama in the last game of the day. Having lost the previous seven straight wagers, the "favorite" bettors wagered with both fists on Arizona. After all, what were the chances of Alabama covering the spread against mighty Arizona? And this would be their last shot at breaking even. So they increased their bets.

Alas, Alabama crushed Arizona, winning by 22 points. I watched as the "favorite" players dragged themselves from their seats, muttering to themselves about how unlucky they'd been. But between you and me, luck had very little to do with it.

They should have been betting less because they were on an obvious losing streak, rather than jeopardizing their entire bankrolls on this last game. Smart gamblers will risk a maximum of six percent of their bankrolls on any one game—on the game they consider they have great value.

And what about the underdog bettors? They should have been progressively increasing their wagers to take advantage of this one-of-a-kind day. Those who didn't actually lost money—the extra money they would've won by increasing their bets while they were winning.

Bet more when you're winning and less when you're losing. And never lose all your money today—tomorrow, there will be another potential play!

2

MONEY MANAGEMENT— MY OPINION!

by Bill Brown

"If you are to become a successful gambler, you must learn money management." How many times have you heard that phrase? If you have ever purchased any gambling books, read any of the quality "free" gaming publications available, or have tuned in to the several gambling TV or radio shows, you are probably tired of hearing it.

But why do you think they keep trying to pound it into our heads? The reason, they tell you (and they are correct), is because poor money management is the downfall of most unsuccessful gamblers.

The question is, "What is proper money management?" The most frequent answer I hear is, "Bet less when you're losing and bet more when you're winning." Do I agree with it? Well, yes and no! How's that for hedging my answer?

Let's start by looking at three football bettors (whom I'll call B1, B2 and B3) at the end of the 2003 season. Each started the season with a bankroll of $10,000. At the end of the season B1 had $9,500; B2 had $14,000; and B3 had $16,000. Can you tell me which had the most successful season? If you said B3, you may or may not be correct. From strictly a financial point, B3 did have the best season, but not necessarily the most successful season. Say what?

Before we can determine which of our players was the most successful, we must look at what their goals were at the beginning of the season. I'll now define them.

187

Player B1 loves to watch football and placed bets mainly for the added excitement involved in having his money on the line. He hoped to win money, of course, but his primary goal was to preserve his bankroll and enjoy the action for the season.

Player B2 is serious about his betting. He put a lot of time and effort into making his wagers and his goal was to end the season with at least a 20 percent return on his original investment.

Player B3 has plenty of money and the $10,000 is not a great amount of money to him. His goal was to win at least $20,000 for the season and he was willing to jeopardize his entire bankroll to do so. So who was the most successful?

If you said B2, you are correct. B2 exceeded his goal by 100 percent. Hoping to win at least $2,000 for the season, he ended up winning $4,000. Next in line for having the most successful season was B1. Although he did not win money, he preserved his bankroll to the extent of losing only $500 (or five percent) while enjoying the season.

The person with the least successful season was B3. Even though he won the most money, he only reached 30 percent of his goal. B3 considers his betting season as mediocre.

What does all this have to do with money management? Well, if these three players came to you before the 2003 season and asked you what type of money management system they should use to have a good chance of reaching their goal, you would not tell all of them, "Bet less when you are losing and bet more when you are winning." This statement may be applicable to B1 and B2, but would not be proper for the goals of B3.

You may also tell B1 to make the same bet on all games (flat betting) all year. Flat betting may be his safest money management system. If he bets $220 a game for 200 games during the season and wins between 48 percent and 55 percent of his wagers, his bankroll will end up anywhere from $6,320 to $12,200. You may also recommend to B2 to vary his wagers according to weights assigned to his plays. His "1 star game" should suggest a bet of only one unit, while his "three star game" should suggest a three unit bet.

This is a little more aggressive style of betting than our original system and may be very profitable as long as our handicapper is accurate in making his star selections. The drawback to this system is if his multi-star selections win less than 50 percent of the time, he may find a serious dent in his bankroll that may be very difficult to overcome.

Another alternative for B2 is to forget the star system and use a slight progressive system when he loses. This will work as long as he picks at around a 50 percent rate and does not reach a situation where he has a high percentage of losses over a period of time. If this happens, he may find his bankroll completely wiped out.

Player B3 has to select a system that will be too volatile for the goals of B1 and B2. He may have to raise his "percentage of bankroll bet" to eight-ten percent, or play a very aggressive money management system, such as the very dangerous Martingale or Grand Martingale systems. Whichever he chooses, he is placing his bankroll in constant jeopardy and may be wiped out in one or two bad weeks.

So what is my opinion on the best money management system? It is my opinion that there are no "best" and there are no "worst" systems. As long as a person understands what the rewards are of a particular money management system and the dangers involved in using that system, his decision to use it is a reasonable one.

Players B1 and B2 would be foolish to try and obtain their goals by the systems used by B3. On the other hand, B3 could probably never reach his goal by using the methods of B1 or B2. Each money management system is correct when used in the proper situation. Each system is wrong when used in an improper situation.

Money management systems should be based on your bankroll and the goals you set for yourself, not on what I or anyone else believes your goals should be. The main thing—and I cannot stress enough how important this is—is that you must understand what the rewards and dangers are before you decide upon a money management system. If you believe the dangers outweigh the rewards of a particular system or don't feel comfortable using it, search for another system, or consider changing your goals.

3

REALITIES OF BEATING THE BOOKIE

Sports betting is one of the wagering opportunities that looks easy, but in reality, is very tough. How come?

Well, first of all sports betting is tough to beat. You are always betting into a negative. That negative is called vigorish. Vigorish is the 10 percent the house charges you when you lose. If you want to win $20, you have to bet $22. If you do win, you get back your $22 plus $20 profit for winning your bet. But if you lose, you lose $22!

Doesn't sound like much, does it?

But you have to win 11 games out of 21 just to break even. That comes out to 52.38 percent. Of course, this doesn't apply to money line games where there is no point spread. Let's look at it another way. Let's say you win 60 percent of your games (though hardly anybody does). If you bet $100 a game and you bet on 100 games, you would win $6,000. You would lose $4,400 and your profit would be $1,600.

Now let's look at it the other way. Let's say you won only 40 percent of your games and lost 60 percent of them. You would have won $4,000, but you would have lost $6,600 for a net loss of $2,600. That's quite a difference in outcome! Some people actually make a living at sports betting. Many, many more have tried and failed. It takes a keen mind, a grasp of situations, and plenty of long hours dedicated to the craft. Also, you must be reality-oriented. You can't expect the unexpected mystery game to bail you out in time of conflict.

The best thing I can tell you is to have fun betting and try to win a couple of bucks. The odds are beatable, but very few can claim they have done it over a long period of time.

CHAPTER 7

PEOPLE IN THE GAME

1

LEM BANKER

One of the hardest ways to make money is through your local bookmaker. Many people have tried; few have succeeded. Out of the few, there is only one I know of who has not only stayed ahead (way ahead!) year in and year out, but has also remained married, raised a family, and has kept a twinkle in his eye. This unique person is Lem Banker.

Many centuries ago, there lived a man named Nostradamus. He had the uncanny ability of predicting the future with an accuracy that amazes people to this day. Banker, a Las Vegas sports betting legend, goes one giant step further—he does it against the pointspread.

"The harder I work, the luckier I get," says Lem, who has been putting in between sixty and seventy hours a week for the past 35 years.

Banker doesn't bet in the traditional sense—instead, he invests. He looks for a certain return on his money. What he really wants is value. He shops for the most advantageous line and wagers accordingly.

"I love Las Vegas. I can't imagine living anywhere else," he told me, "because here I can shop at over 45 sportsbooks." A half-point here, a middle there, can make a big difference in your weekly total. When you buy a car, you always go to a few dealers. When you bet sports, it's a good idea to do the same.

Discipline is one of the most important weapons in any sports bettor's arsenal. You simply have to pick your shots. As Lem likes to say, "They play the Star Spangled Banner every day; there will always be another game tomorrow. If the price or situation isn't right, pass on the game. Make a 'mind bet.' After all, the worst you can do is lose your mind!"

The telephone rings constantly in his spacious home; information in, information out. A lot of the time, he has one phone in his ear while speaking with someone else on another phone. When Lem talks, people listen.

He picked the money winner in 21 out of the first 24 Super Bowl games. In the background is a teletype machine keeping him updated on games in progress and what's going on.

"The only thing I bet on is people," Lem says. He doesn't bet on dice, cards or horses. For a guy who works so hard, he is extremely generous with his picks. As long as he had made his wagers at his price, Lem is happy to share his "homework" with friends. He's like the brainy student who lets you copy his answers before history class.

Banker works out daily on his punching bag and free weights in his home gym. He is in great physical and emotional health. In the heat of the action, he can sometimes be found in one of his two saunas.

"The odds are more in your favor to become a rock star or a movie star than to make a living at sports betting" he claims. But we've included a few tips from the "Sage of the Strip" on the next page to help you.

Lem Banker has his feet firmly planted on the ground. That's an amazing statement in itself, considering the quicksand nature of sports gambling. This man is a winner in a town filled with should-have-beens. There are a lot of wise guys in Las Vegas; Lem Banker is a wise man.

5 Steps to Making Money on Sports Betting

1. Bet against public opinion.

2. Do not try to play catch-up by increasing your wagers when you are losing.

3. Increase your wagers when you are winning.

4. What you save is what you earn. Shop, shop, shop!

5. Be prepared. Do your homework. Read and gather your information.

6. Bet only two-percent to five-percent of your bankroll on any one game.

7. Don't be afraid to pass on a game. There will be another one tomorrow.

8. Don't bet a game just because it's on television.

2

SONNY REIZNER

Sonny is the perfect name for a guy who is filled with laughter, wit and a lifetime of experience he will generously share. He is more than just another piece in the crazy quilt of Las Vegas. He's a legend. Better yet, he is accessible. One walks away richer for having spent any moment of time with this man. His name is Sonny Reizner.

Reizner grew up in Taunton, Massachusetts, less than an hour from Cape Cod—but more importantly, less than half-an-hour from Fenway Park, a geographical piece of fate that would prove to be formative. Always a sports fan, Sonny made his first wager when he was fifteen years old, taking the short end: he bet $9 to win $20 on the Boston Braves when they were two runs down early in the game. He won his bet. Little did he know at the time that the seed of the future was firmly planted in the fertile soil of his mind.

A few years came and went with Sonny dabbling in betting sports, but mostly finding his way through those glorious years in which young men often find out who they are. In and out of the Air Force, he was a "link trainer" instructor, teaching officers blind instrument flying.

On a visit to Miami, Sonny met the woman who would become his wife and mother of their four children. "Rolene was looking for a rich guy and I was looking for a beautiful girl. We ended up settling for each other," he recalls with a laugh. Sonny and Rolene tried several types of endeavors. Considering his early betting success and his penchant for information and action, "endeavors" was a huge underdog.

"The trouble was that regular enterprises always interfered with gambling. I went to Northeastern for a year

198

and was earning all A's, but found myself running to the pay phone to make my 12:30 p.m. bets. Unfortunately, I was picking all losers at this point, so I had to make a choice." Academia's loss was to become gambling's gain.

Traveling to Miami for the Grapefruit League circuit, he bet baseball, jai alai, and even the dogs. Sonny speaks fondly of the brains of the betting group he was involved with at that time when they were wagering on dogs.

"The guy was amazing. He had such an affinity for dogs, we used to kid him and suggest that he raised his leg when he had to relieve himself." Each winter for several years, the fraternity of bettors would meet and gamble at Greenacres in Miami.

One year Sonny was on a miserable losing streak as the trip was approaching. He bet five games to get even. Unfortunately, all five lost and Sonny lost his desire to frolic on the beach. A few weeks later, he got a phone call from one of the guys he traditionally met, asking him why he hadn't made the trip. When Sonny told him how bad he'd been running, the guy answered, "You're lucky—it rained all week!" Some luck!

A few weeks later, Reizner received a telephone call that would forever change his life. An acquaintance that worked for Bob Martin at the Churchill Downs Race and Sportsbook in Las Vegas was moving back east to live. Bob was going to need some help.

Sonny moved to Las Vegas and hasn't looked back since. He took to the land of neon like a fish to water. Under the tutelage of Martin and later Lou Kopple, Reizner learned his lessons well. Only trouble was, his betting interfered with his job and vice-versa. The different decisions that were expected of him were tearing him in opposite directions. He had to make another decision: it was all or nothing. So gambling at the sportsbook took a back seat to working behind the window.

In a few years, Sonny's perseverance and wits paid off in a sportsbook manager's position under Bill Friedman at the late, great Castaways Hotel & Casino.

It didn't take long for Sonny to make his mark. Within a couple of years, he created the "Castaways Challenge," the first football contest ever staged in Nevada. It was such an immediate success that the following year, 1979, he not only repeated the Castaways Challenge, but he also added the "Ultimate Challenge." More action, more interest, more money.

By now, people in the industry had not only heard of this "hole in the wall" sportsbook at the Castaways run by Sonny Reizner, they also began to follow his every move. He was considered to be the maverick innovator of his time: the only person who could outdo Sonny was Sonny himself! He soon came out with the "Monday Night Fever Card," a proposition parlay card that cemented his legend before the ink on the cards was dry.

He knew it was a major success when he printed a replica of the card in the *Las Vegas Review Journal*, and people cut it out and jammed the sportsbook with their selections. Sonny then began to give out T-shirts and the people loved them. Within a few days, he had thousands of walking billboards all over town. Like Midas, everything Sonny Reizner touched turned to gold.

But nothing could have prepared him for the success he achieved when he made a line on "Who shot J.R.?" at the height of the "Dallas" television show's popularity. Calls of inquiry came from every corner of the country. Telephones at the Castaways were ringing off the hook.

Reporters all wanted to write about the guy who put out the line. Sonny handled the hubbub with his usual good humor and graciousness. He knew how to get a good thing going, and also possessed that most rare of skills—he knew how to keep it going. Eventually, the Nevada Gaming

YOU CAN BET ON IT!

Control Board made a ruling that there could be no betting on an event unless it was decided on the field of play. The crazy bets were put to a quick halt, but not before the Castaways expanded as the result of the publicity brought in by Sonny. "I'm proud to say that they enlarged the Hole-in-the-Wall sportsbook twice. First time it was from 19 feet to 20 feet; then from 20 feet to 21 feet."

On the sacred land once occupied by the Castaways now sits the Mirage. Larger yes; more beautiful, definitely! But there was something indefinable about the Castaways. Like an old, dear friend who is lost forever, it still has the timeless power to evoke emotions about a time that was.

Next for Sonny Reizner was a brief stint at the Frontier as executive director of sports gaming. Then an offer that he couldn't refuse: To be a consultant in the construction and planning of the Rio Suites Hotel and Casino's race and sportsbook. This appointment would become the high water mark of a career that few men in his industry would ever achieve.

Sonny's face would light up when he recalled the designing and free reign he was accorded in making the kind of sports and race book he himself would want to frequent. Next to the airy book is a deli aptly named Sonny's Deli. "I can always serve sandwiches if I don't make it as a sportsbook director," he used to kid. Not much chance of that! He has a following much like a performer. People liked his style and the way he treated them. After all, it takes a bettor to know what a bettor wants.

During the 1990-91 football season, Sonny was one of the many sportsbook directors who appeared on a local television news and sports show to give their weekend picks. The weekly segment soon became a cult classic and kept building to the playoffs and Super Bowl. Reizner picked his way into the championship round where he faced Art Manteris of the Las Vegas Hilton, who had also earned his way through formidable challengers to reach the finals. Both Sonny and Art had posted in their books Reizner as a decided underdog (no, you couldn't bet on it), ranging from +160 at the Rio to +200 at the Hilton.

As though preordained by the "Gods of Gambling," Sonny took the New York Giants and Art took the Buffalo Bills. After the game, Art called to congratulate Sonny and reminded him that he could collect the dinner they had bet. Reizner, being a shrewd percentage man for most of his five decades, reminded Art that since he was posted as a 2-1 dog, he was entitled to two dinners! You have to wake up pretty early to slip something by him.

Sonny and Rolene continued to enjoy life in Las Vegas. He moved on to the Sheraton Desert Inn as race and sportsbook director. Their four children are grown up and are engaged in successful careers of their own: their daughters Gale and Jan are school teachers; their son Adam owns a landscaping business in Las Vegas; and their son Alan is a drummer in California. Sadly, however, Sonny passed away on November 30, 2002.

Those of us who knew Sonny Reizner know that he was more than an astute merchandiser, and more than an excellent sportsbook director. He was one of those rare breeds of people who would offer you a handshake and look you in the eye. He would share a laugh and make you feel that something special had just occurred. He was the kind of person who enriched all the lives he touched.

He was the best of the Las Vegas that used to be, and set the standard for the Las Vegas that is. Like fine wine, he continued to get better. Simply put, Mr. Reizner made the day Sonny.

3

ANDREW ISKOE

Predicting the future based on statistics from the past has always been a passion for Andrew Iskoe. He graduated from the University of Pennsylvania's Wharton School of Business, and with that piece of parchment, he could have set himself up for life shuffling papers and making profits for stockholders. Instead, Iskoe chose to become a professional sports handicapper. We began our interview sitting outside a Downtown Las Vegas casino on a sunny spring day.

Larry Grossman: When did you begin handicapping sports?

Andrew Iskoe: I began in junior high school, but I have been a sports fan from as far back as I can remember. I started with football power ratings in my early teens. I grew up in New York and kept detailed statistics on the Mets and Yankees batting averages, which I would update everyday. After a while, I refined my approach and began to handicap in a more structured way.

LG: What is the challenge of handicapping for you?

AI: Uncovering the relationships between past performance and probable future performance is what I find most fascinating. It takes a great deal of creativity and analysis, but the reward comes in almost instant gratification. The feedback is there immediately, and it allows me to make the proper adjustments.

LG: Why did you decide to settle in Las Vegas?

AI: After graduating from college in 1976, I worked in corporate taxation for the insurance industry. I lived and worked in Rhode Island and Arkansas before moving to Las

Vegas. In 1982, I began putting together a weekly newsletter, *The Logical Approach*, during football season.

I also began to publish a series of books titled *The Pointspread Encyclopedia*, which allowed the football handicapper to research trends and angles in football. These books were enthusiastically received in Las Vegas. A few years passed, and there came that moment in time when I decided to legally practice what I preached. That's when I moved to Las Vegas. I also believed it would be beneficial for me to live in a betting environment where I could share in the experiences and knowledge of my fellow handicappers.

LG: Of all the sports that you handicap, which is the most—and the least—predictable to you?

AI: Strangely enough, I've had the most success in pro football, which many people believe is the most difficult of all sports. College football has proven much more difficult for me.

LG: What are some of the things you've learned over the years?

AI: I like to back good teams. They have the capability to play their best on a much more consistent basis. I'd rather go down with a good favorite than bet on a bad underdog that has to raise their level of performance.

Baseball, once it gets to the sixth or seventh week of the season, becomes a relatively predictable game. Of course, baseball is starting-pitcher driven. As a rule, you'll see fewer cold pitchers getting hot as the season moves on, than hot pitchers getting cold. Baseball is wagered by using the money line rather than the pointspread, so using proper money management is even more critical in this sport than in others.

LG: What advice on money management would you suggest to bettors?

AI: Money management actually has two stages: the first is the accumulation of a bankroll, and then there is the growth of that bankroll. You have to get your initial seed money from somewhere, whether it is from an unrelated business or somewhere else.

Sometimes, a bettor will try to get their initial bankroll from a small amount of money that they bet very aggressively in the beginning. I begin the season with a set amount of money and a game plan. I gear my season based on what made me successful in the past. Was it straight plays or totals, parlays or run line plays?

I especially like to parlay big favorites in baseball. It's the one situation where I find a parlay very advantageous for me. I like to play the run line, laying the run and a half. Parlaying underdogs can be both greedy and foolish. If you win one and lose one, you still win money if you bet them straight up. Also, I suggest betting on the football team that you think will win the game outright. Four out of five times, the pointspread doesn't even come into play.

LG: How do changes in the rules affect your handicapping?

AI: Before the changes happen, you can only speculate on what might occur, based on logic. To get a true understanding, you have to see what happens during the course of a season.

Obviously, the three-point shot in basketball had a major effect on "total" players. It has also allowed weaker teams in college basketball to recruit a different type of player. Traditionally, the smaller schools get blown out by 20 to 30 points by the major powers. In many respects, the three-point shot has kept the games closer.

LG: What advice would you give to someone who is just getting started?

AI: Be patient, be realistic, be creative. Success doesn't come overnight. We all must learn from our mistakes.

Sports handicapping is like a scientist's laboratory, always experimenting, tinkering, adjusting and refining our methods. The pursuit of the ultimate success formula is both exhilarating and wrought with frustration.

But the rewards of your hard work, research, and dedication will pay you back many times over. Just keep plugging away.

4

LOU KOPPLE

Certain people make a difference in the lives they touch. They move along the road of life with a purpose. Although the twists and turns make some days a roller coaster ride, they determinedly stay the course with the intelligence and honesty that escape many people. Such a man was Lou Kopple.

Being around this gentleman simply enriched your own sense of self-worth. He was a tapestry of historical significance. As a youngster, Kopple was a bat boy for the Chicago White Sox. He would shag flies with future Hall of Fame inductees. He witnessed Babe Ruth calling his shot in the 1932 World Series. He saw Ty Cobb sharpen his spikes on the dugout steps to intimidate the opposing team. His eyes have seen the glory.

Lou Kopple has always had the gamble in him. He grew up in a tough area of Chicago where he learned to play craps at an early age. One day, when he was supposed to be in school, his father caught him on his knees shooting craps.

"I can still feel the smack on the side of my head that my father doled out to end this particular session," he recalled. Lou would speak of his parents in almost reverential tones. The respect he had for them, although they were long departed, still burned brightly within him.

In 1971, Kopple moved to Las Vegas so he could legally get in on the action he enjoys so much. As a veteran gambler, he knew the advantage of being able to shop around and find the best price available.

In those days, you could go into a sportsbook and all sorts of Damon Runyan characters were everywhere. It used to look like central casting for a black and white cellblock movie. The images still remain intact to some extent, but day-by-day it changed to a more pristine environment.

Back then, you could walk into a sportsbook and the ball game could be in the fourth inning with the home team ahead 4-1, and the guy behind the counter would quote you a price. These were gambling times and the men in charge had to think fast on their feet. The only painted line was found on the turnpike. One thing led to another and fate brought Lou Kopple to the other side of the counter. He managed and opened many of the sportsbooks in Las Vegas. He was part of the team that opened the first sportsbook in a major hotel, the Stardust. Lou broke in many of the guys who eventually would become managers in their own right.

One of them was Sonny Reizner, former race and sportsbook director at the gone-but-not-forgotten Castaways Hotel. Sonny was the one who introduced me to Lou. Although it was many months ago, when you meet an individual like Lou who impresses you on many different levels simultaneously, you tend to remember those feelings—emotions that can best be described as genuine and warm, with the seed of friendship firmly planted.

Sonny often recalled working for Lou in a way that is an equal mixture of love and respect. "Lou Kopple is the greatest guy I ever worked for," he would say. "He was always fair and you always knew where you stood."

Reizner told a great story about the kind of guy Kopple was behind the counter. "There was this player who came in and played a four-team baseball parlay and three of the games had already won. He made a pretty substantial bet and stood to make a hefty score.

"Before the last game began, he walked up to Lou and showed him his ticket. Excitedly, he vowed that if he won, he would give Lou $500, if Lou would help root for his team. But Lou refused so as not to betray a trust. Of course, it didn't matter if Lou rooted or not: it was just Lou's way of rising above. There wasn't a shadow of a doubt as to where he stood." Sonny added, "Lou Kopple is a one-of-a-kind man and I think the world of him."

Lou retired, but he still spent a great deal of time in the sportsbooks around town; most often, he was at the baby he helped nurture, the Stardust. He couldn't go anywhere without someone saying hello or offering a big handshake.

I was fortunate enough to befriend Lou Kopple. He was the type of person who didn't have to say anything; but in his introspection, there was such a strong foundation of honesty and integrity, it seemed to shout out to those who cared to listen.

Lou has since passed away, but he was a link to those glorious days of Ruth and Cobb and the openings of the sportsbooks in the hotels of Las Vegas. He lived through the golden age of this country and, more specifically, of Las Vegas. He walked tall, as a man with value and integrity should.

"I've been betting since I was nine years old," Lou once said. "Every day," he added, without missing a beat. All I know is that this world would be a warmer, fundamentally better place if we could all wake up one day and somehow magically be blessed with a residue of Lou Kopple's grace and sense of being.

Lou was quite a man!

5

HOWARD SCHWARTZ

All the gamblers I know who are remotely successful in Las Vegas are avid readers. This is no coincidence; one of the key aspects of gambling is an understanding of the game you are going to play or the sports event you're going to wager on.

What is gambling if not the exercise of making the correct bet at the right time? Of course, money management is also important and should always be considered in your betting equation. But where can you learn about gambling and money management without having your lessons cost you an arm and a leg? I'm about to tell you.

There's a gem of a bookstore totally dedicated to the gambling enthusiast. Almost every title on its shelves is devoted to some aspect of gambling. Whether you're a beginner or a world champion, they have a book for you.

The Gambler's Book Shop is a smorgasbord for your mind. Located at 630 South 11th Street near downtown Las Vegas, it is one of the truly great specialty stores in the world. Obviously, they're doing something right.

In addition to their walk-in trade, the Gambler's Book Shop has cultivated a mail order business that ships books, tapes and computer gaming software all over the world. You can obtain a free catalog by calling 1-800-634-6243.

In the store, as in the catalog, you'll find thousands of titles to choose from. They also feature a used book section in the store that offers substantial discounts to gamblers who want to save a few bucks for the tables.

The real star of the store comes in the form of a character named Howard Schwartz. This man is a walking, talking computer! Formerly a member of the University of Northern Colorado faculty, Schwartz's understanding and memory are nothing short of amazing. He seems to have complete recall of his immense inventory, and is probably the foremost authority on gambling books and systems in the world.

Schwartz has been with the Gambler's Book Shop for over fifteen years. The honesty and competence he shows customers is legendary. Howard doesn't sell—he helps. Someone could get very rich if they could figure out a way to clone him.

When I used to visit Las Vegas (before I moved here), there were so many things to do, time flew by—it seemed as though, as soon as I arrived, it was time to pack up and leave. Before the time flies by for you, do yourself a favor and visit the Gambler's Book Shop. Believe me, it will be time well spent. After all, you are what you read.

6

MIKE LEE

Mike Lee was a lot different than most of the people who bet sports. It's not that he was a college graduate (University of Alabama), or that he wrote country music. No, the thing that makes Mike Lee so different was that he's a winner.

Many people try to beat sports betting. Very few succeed and even fewer flourish. Mike has become a mini-industry unto himself. He published the *Moneymaker*, a college and pro football-handicapping newsletter that comes out each week during the football season. Serious football bettors seek it out.

Lee has earned his stripes and his reputation. He won the prestigious Castaways Ultimate Challenge in 1985. Also, he has finished in the top 10 percent of just about every handicapping contest he has entered. In 1989, he won the Hilton Superbook contest with a 75-win, 37-loss record, winning $114,000 in competition against the best football handicapping minds in the country.

As a child growing up in Georgia, Mike had a keen interest in probability and chance. He would flip a coin for hours, recording the results and trying to figure out what was to be learned. A short while later, he discovered Stratomatic baseball and he further honed his strategy and probability skills. In 1972, Mike picked up a football publication from a company named Leedo Pix in Bluebell, Pennsylvania. He contacted them, and credits Leo Minnucci for being his mentor and for cultivating his general interest into something more specific.

Lee moved to Las Vegas in 1978 with the dream of becoming a handicapper and writing a newsletter. For motivation, he stared at a photograph that he prominently displayed in his home: a photo of a former Castaways handicapping champion clutching a bunch of cash and a trophy, emblematic of a true winner.

While still perfecting his craft, he was approached with an offer to write a book on baseball handicapping. The fruit of his labor was *Betting the Bases*, which continues to be the most sought after and quoted baseball-handicapping book ever published. (The gentleman who approached Mike was John Luckman who, along with his wife Edna, founded The Gambler's Book Shop in Las Vegas.)

In 1983, Mike founded Mike Lee Sports, a handicapping newsletter and service that assists the bettor with information that Mike cultivates by poring over information and computer data.

"Today, it's much tougher to handicap without a computer," he once asserted. "Logging the games by hand takes up a lot of time and, after all, there are just so many hours in the day. The computer is my 'runner.' It frees up my time and allows me to devote all my energy to handicapping the games."

Mike liked to "play" college football more than professional because, "You simply have more to choose from. I certainly enjoy pro football and the contests, but the college game offers more opportunity."

He continued, "The really good handicappers are underdog bettors, but obviously you must know when to bet the favorites. You certainly can't do anything exclusively when you make a wager. I think, to be successful, you have to be primarily an underdog handicapper with an eye out for favorites that come along."

Another key to handicapping football, Mike would say, is to "look for a team that plays good defense. Defense keeps you in the ball game." Many times, a team that is sputtering offensively, but has a strong defense, will keep the score close enough so that in the latter part of the game, they will give "your team" the opportunity to cover the point spread.

Lee had a glimmer in his eye when asked about the coming football season. It's the time of year when he felt the most at home, crunching statistics and handicapping football games.

Before his tragic passing on September 8, 2004, Mike no longer flipped coins and charted their probability. Long ago, he had put aside his beloved Stratomatic baseball game. But like a major league baseball player who took a million grounders in the little leagues, the practice and the effort made the man better and wiser for the experience,

7

ABOUT THE GUEST COLUMNISTS

Lem Banker is a professional sports handicapper and bettor who earns his living wagering on sports. He is the co-author of *Sports Betting*, and appears regularly on radio and television sports shows. Banker also writes columns on winning strategies for sports bettors for several gaming publications

Bill Brown is a Las Vegas computer expert. It took him five years to complete his research for *190 Million Hands Of Blackjack*, a classic in the field. Using multiple charts and tables, he examines the reliability of basic strategy, including single and multiple deck play. Brown has written columns for numerous gambling publications.

Rommy Faversham is an author and speaker on thoroughbred horseracing. A graduate of the University of Southern California School of Medicine, Dr. Faversham was the turf correspondent for Larry Grossman's radio talk show for many years and has been published in *American Turf Monthly* and *Western Gambler*.

Andrew Iskoe is a professional sports handicapper who owns *The Logical Approach*, a sports betting newsletter. He is also the author of *The Pointspread Encyclopedia* series. The co-host of "Insomniac Sports" on The American Sports Radio Network, he is a graduate of the University of Pennsylvania, Wharton School of Business.

The late **Mike Lee** was the founder of Mike Lee Sports and the author of *Betting The Bases*, *Mindbetting and Basketball Handicapping*. Lee won the two most prestigious football-handicapping contests in Las Vegas: the Hilton's Superbook Contest and the Castaways' Ultimate Challenge.

Vincent Magliulo was race and sportsbook director at Caesars Palace in Las Vegas. He is a native of Brooklyn, New York, who has been in the sports betting industry for numerous years. He has also instructed classes in Sportsbook Management for Community College of Southern Nevada.

The late **Mort Olshan** is a legend in the world of sports handicapping. He founded *The Gold Sheet* in 1957, and also originated the concept of football handicapping seminars. The author of *Winning Theories of Sports Handicapping, The Competitors Creed*, and *The Best Of The Gold Sheet*, no one is more respected in the betting industry.

The late **Sonny Reizner** gained fame as race and sportsbook director of The Hole In The Wall sportsbook at the Castaways in Las Vegas. He also was sportsbook director at the Sheraton Desert Inn in Las Vegas, a position he has also held at the Rio Suites. Reizner is the co-author of *Sports Betting With Sonny Reizner* and *How To Be A Winning Sports Bettor*, an audiotape.

Michael "Roxy" Roxborough was the president of Las Vegas Sports Consultants, Inc., which was the world's largest independent odds making firm. His company provided odds and consultations to over thirty legal sportsbooks in Nevada. Roxborough is the author of *Race and Sports Book Management*, and his newspaper column, *American's Line*, is nationally syndicated.

The late **Tex Sheahan**, was the "dean of poker columnists." He grew up in Chicago and began his gambling career as a boy pitching pennies. He is the author of *Gambling with The Best Of 'Em!* Sheahan had been writing gambling columns for many years, and has been published in most of the nation's gaming magazines, including *Card Player*.

Chuck Sippl is a senior editor and partner in *The Gold Sheet*. He is a regular guest on Larry Grossman's radio show,

You Can Bet On It where he shares insights and analyses on football and basketball betting. A summa cum laude graduate of the University of California, Irvine, Sippl was the sports writer and editor at KFWB radio for twelve years.

Bryan Leonard is in his 19th season as a Professional Handicapper. He is the publisher of the highly successful *Pigskin Report Football Newsletter* as well as the owner of www.FootballWinners.com. He is a sought after guest for numerous handicapping radio shows as well as acclaimed contests including The Stardust Invitational.

Micha Roberts is the Director of Race & Sports Operations for Station Casinos in Las Vegas, NV. He writes a weekly NASCAR column for *Gaming Today* and VegasInsider.com that gives insight and observations for the weeks' upcoming race.

Jeff Sherman came to Las Vegas in 1993 after graduating from UCSB with a degree in Business Economics. He started immediately in the race and sports industry at the Imperial Palace and worked as a ticket writer for 2 years while attending UNLV for an MBA. While at the Imperial Palace, he was promoted to supervisor. After a 6 year stint at the Imperial Palace, Jeff took his skills to the Regent Las Vegas for 2 years and then moved on to help open the Palms, remaining there for 2 1/2 years. In 2004, Jeff joined the race and sports book staff as the assistant manager at the Las Vegas Hilton. He operates his golf website as golfodds.com.

Steve Fezzik is a professional handicapper and Bettor who was the runner up at the 2003 Stardust Invitational Handicapping Tournament. He is a frequent writer for the sportsbetting website www.therx.com. He can be reached at fezziksplace.com.

Fred Crespi has set up shop as Race and Sports Book Manager at the Palms Casino Resort in Las Vegas, Nevada for the last two years. Fred moved to Nevada in 1993, following a four year stint at the University of Colorado at Boulder, where he successfully completed his undergraduate degree in International Affairs. His love of sports and handicapping brought him to Nevada, where he started his career at Boulder Station in August of 1994. Fred moved into management in late 1996, with his first promotion to department manager in 1998. A two year stint at Sunset Station soon followed for Fred in 2000 before heading to The Palms Casino Resort in August of 2002.

Larry Grossman is the host and producer of *You Can Bet On It*. His radio show features interviews with gaming authors, sports handicappers, sportsbook directors, World Champion poker players and famous gamblers. The show began in 1989 and helped to establish him as a gaming analyst who can be counted on for accurate information, honesty and integrity. The show is broadcast in Las Vegas and can be heard on the internet at www.larrygrossman.com Grossman also has a regular column on gaming tips which appears in *What's On* magazine in Las Vegas.

He is also a devoted fan of the World Series of Poker, which he has photographed each year since 1988. His photographs are on permanent displays at the Sunset Station poker room and at the Gambler's Book Shop in Las Vegas. His photographs have appeared on many poker book covers and have been featured in *Card Player* Magazine and *Esquire* Magazine.

THE CHAMPIONSHIP SERIES
POWERFUL BOOKS YOU MUST HAVE

CHAMPIONSHIP TOURNAMENT POKER by Tom McEvoy. New Cardoza Edition! Rated by pros as best book on tournaments ever written and enthusiastically endorsed by more than five world champions, this is the definitive guide to winning tournaments and a must for every player's library. McEvoy lets you in on the secrets he has used to win millions of dollars in tournaments and the insights he has learned competing against the best players in the world. Packed solid with winning strategies for all 11 games in the World Series of Poker, with extensive discussions of 7-card stud, limit hold'em, pot and no-limit hold'em, Omaha high-low, re-buy, half-half tournaments, satellites, and strategies for each stage of tournaments. Tons of essential concepts and specific strategies jam-pack the book. Phil Hellmuth, 1989 WSOP champion says, "[this] is the world's most definitive guide to winning poker tournaments." 416 pages, paperback, $29.95.

CHAMPIONSHIP TABLE (at the World Series of Poker) by Dana Smith, Ralph Wheeler, and Tom McEvoy. New Cardoza Edition! From 1970 when the champion was presented a silver cup, to the present when the champion was awarded more than $2 million, *Championship Table* celebrates three decades of poker greats who have competed to win poker's most coveted title. This book gives you the names and photographs of all the players who made the final table, pictures of the last hand the champion played against the runner-up, how they played their cards, and how much they won. This book also features fascinating interviews and conversations with the champions and runners-up and interesting highlights from each Series. This is a fascinating and invaluable resource book for WSOP and gaming buffs. In some cases the champion himself wrote "how it happened," as did two-time champion Doyle Brunson when Stu Ungar caught a wheel in 1980 on the turn to deprive "Texas Dolly" of his third title. Includes tons of vintage photographs. 208 pages, paperback, $19.95.

CHAMPIONSHIP SATELLITE STRATEGY by Brad Daugherty & Tom McEvoy. In 2002 and 2003, satellite players won their way into the $10,000 WSOP buy-in and emerged as champions, winning more than $2 million each. You can too! You'll learn specific, proven strategies for winning almost any satellite. Learn the ten ways to win a seat at the WSOP and other big tournaments, how to win limit hold'em and no-limit hold'em satellites, one-table satellites for big tournaments, and online satellites, plus how to play the final table of super satellites. McEvoy and Daugherty sincerely believe that if you practice these strategies, you can win your way into any tournament for a fraction of the buy-in. You'll learn how much to bet, how hard to pressure opponents, how to tell when an opponent is bluffing, how to play deceptively, and how to use your chips as weapons of destruction. Includes a special chapter on no-limit hold'em satellites! 256 pages. Illustrated hands, photos, glossary. $24.95.

CHAMPIONSHIP PRACTICE HANDS by T.J. Cloutier & Tom McEvoy. Two tournament legends show you how to become a winning tournament player. Get inside their heads as they think their way through the correct strategy at 57 limit and no-limit practice hands. Cloutier and McEvoy show you how to use your skill and intuition to play strategic hands for maximum profit in real tournament scenarios and how 45 key hands were played by champions in turnaround situations at the WSOP. By sharing their analysis on how the winners and losers played key hands, you'll gain tremendous insights into how tournament poker is played at the highest levels. Learn how champions think and how they play major hands in strategic tournament situations, Cloutier and McEvoy believe that you will be able to win your share of the profits in today's tournaments—and join them at the championship table far sooner than you ever imagined. 288 pages, illustrated with card pictures, $29.95

THE CHAMPIONSHIP SERIES
POWERFUL BOOKS YOU MUST HAVE

CHAMPIONSHIP OMAHA (Omaha High-Low, Pot-limit Omaha, Limit High Omaha) by Tom McEvoy & T.J. Cloutier. Clearly-written strategies and powerful advice from Cloutier and McEvoy who have won four World Series of Poker titles in Omaha tournaments. Powerful advice shows you how to win at low-limit and high-stakes games, how to play against loose and tight opponents, and the differing strategies for rebuy and freezeout tournaments. Learn the best starting hands, when slowplaying a big hand is dangerous, what danglers are and why winners don't play them, why pot-limit Omaha is the only poker game where you sometimes fold the nuts on the flop and are correct in doing so and overall, and how you can win a lot of money at Omaha! 230 pages, photos, illustrations, $39.95. Now only $29.95!

CHAMPIONSHIP STUD (Seven-Card Stud, Stud 8/or Better and Razz) by Dr. Max Stern, Linda Johnson, and Tom McEvoy. The authors, who have earned millions of dollars in major tournaments and cash games, eight World Series of Poker bracelets and hundreds of other titles in competition against the best players in the world show you the winning strategies for medium-limit side games as well as poker tournaments and a general tournament strategy that is applicable to any form of poker. Includes give-and-take conversations between the authors to give you more than one point of view on how to play poker. 200 pages, hand pictorials, photos. $39.95.

CHAMPIONSHIP HOLD'EM by Tom McEvoy & T.J. Cloutier. Hard-hitting hold'em the way it's played today in both limit cash games and tournaments. Get killer advice on how to win more money in rammin'-jammin' games, kill-pot, jackpot, shorthanded, and other types of cash games. You'll learn the thinking process before the flop, on the flop, on the turn, and at the river with specific suggestions for what to do when good or bad things happen plus 20 illustrated hands with play-by-play analyses. Specific advice for rocks in tight games, weaklings in loose games, experts in solid games, how hand values change in jackpot games, when you should fold, check, raise, reraise, check-raise, slowplay, bluff, and tournament strategies for small buy-in, big buy-in, rebuy, incremental add-on, satellite and big-field major tournaments. Wow! Easy-to-read and conversational, if you want to become a lifelong winner at limit hold'em, you need this book! 388 Pages, Illustrated, Photos. $39.95. Now only $29.95!

CHAMPIONSHIP NO-LIMIT & POT-LIMIT HOLD'EM by T.J. Cloutier & Tom McEvoy. New Cardoza Edition! The definitive guide to winning at two of the world's most exciting poker games! Written by eight time World Champion players T.J. Cloutier (1998 and 2002 Player of the Year) and Tom McEvoy (the foremost author on tournament strategy) who have won millions of dollars each playing no-limit and pot-limit hold'em in cash games and major tournaments around the world. You'll get all the answers here—no holds barred—to your most important questions: How do you get inside your opponents' heads and learn how to beat them at their own game? How can you tell how much to bet, raise, and reraise in no-limit hold'em? When can you bluff? How do you set up your opponents in pot-limit hold'em so you can win a monster pot? What are the best strategies for winning no-limit and pot-limit tournaments, satellites, and supersatellites? You get rock-solid and inspired advice from two of the most recognizable figures in poker—advice that you can bank on. If you want to become a winning player, and a champion, you must have this book. 304 pages, paperback, illustrations, photos. $29.95

POWERFUL POKER SIMULATIONS

A MUST FOR SERIOUS PLAYERS WITH A COMPUTER!
IBM compatibles CD ROM Win 95, 98, 2000, NT, ME, XP - Full
Color Graphics

These incredible full color poker simulation programs are the absolute best method to improve your game. Computer opponents play like real players. All games let you set the limits and rake, have fully programmable players, adjustable lineup, stat tracking, and Hand Analyzer for starting hands. Mike Caro, the world's foremost poker theoretician says, "Amazing... a steal for under $500... get it, it's great." Includes free telephone support. "Smart Advisor" gives expert advice for every play in every game!

NEW!
Windows Versions
More Features!

1. TURBO TEXAS HOLD'EM FOR WINDOWS - $89.95 - Choose which players, how many, 2-10, you want to play, create loose/tight game, control check-raising, bluffing, position, sensitivity to pot odds, more! Also, instant replay, pop-up odds, Professional Advisor, keeps track of play statistics. Free bonus: Hold'em Hand Analyzer analyzes all 169 pocket hands in detail, their win rates under any conditions you set. Caro says this "hold'em software is the most powerful ever created." Great product!

2. TURBO SEVEN-CARD STUD FOR WINDOWS - $89.95 - Create any conditions of play; choose number of players (2-8), bet amounts, fixed or spread limit, bring-in method, tight/loose conditions, position, reaction to board, number of dead cards, stack deck to create special conditions, instant replay. Terrific stat reporting includes analysis of starting cards, 3-D bar charts, graphs. Play interactively, run high speed simulation to test strategies. Hand Analyzer analyzes starting hands in detail. Wow!

3. TURBO OMAHA HIGH-LOW SPLIT FOR WINDOWS - $89.95 -Specify any playing conditions; betting limits, number of raises, blind structures, button position, aggressiveness/passiveness of opponents, number of players (2-10), types of hands dealt, blinds, position, board reaction, specify flop, turn, river cards! Choose opponents, use provided point count or create your own. Statistical reporting, instant replay, pop-up odds, high speed simulation to test strategies, amazing Hand Analyzer, much more!

4. TURBO OMAHA HIGH FOR WINDOWS - $89.95 - Same features as above, but tailored for Omaha High-only. Caro says program is "an electrifying research tool... it can clearly be worth thousands of dollars to any serious player. A must for Omaha High players.

5. TURBO 7 STUD 8 OR BETTER - $89.95 - Brand new with all the features you expect from the Wilson Turbo products: the latest artificial intelligence, instant advice and exact odds, play versus 2-7 opponents, enhanced data charts that can be exported or printed, the ability to fold out of turn and immediately go to the next hand, ability to peek at opponents hand, optional warning mode that warns you if a play disagrees with the advisor, and automatic testing mode that can run up to 50 tests unattended. Challenge tough computer players who vary their styles for a truly great poker game.

6. TOURNAMENT TEXAS HOLD'EM - $59.95 Set-up for tournament practice and play, this realistic simulation pits you against celebrity look-alikes. Tons of options let you control tournament size with 10 to 300 entrants, select limits, ante, rake, blind structures, freezeouts, number of rebuys and competition level of opponents - average, tough, or toughest. Pop-up status report shows how you're doing vs. the competition. Save tournaments in progress to play again later. Additional feature allows you to quickly finish a folded hand and go on to the next.

Order Toll-Free 1-800-577-WINS or go to www.cardozapub.com

GET 57% OFF SUBSCRIPTION!!!

Check out Avery Cardoza's new gambling lifestyle magazine. It is loaded with articles, columns, how-to information, and so much more—everything you need and want to know about the exciting world of gambling. And it's here now: PLAYER magazine!

Everyone is talking about PLAYER, which has turned into the hottest new magazine launch in a decade. Our first issue alone was featured on three national television shows (The View, Inside Edition, and Conan O'Brien), national radio (ESPN), and national print (such as Newsweek), unprecedented coverage for an independent launch. Why is PLAYER so hot? In two words: gambling lifestyle—drinking, smoking, dining, entertainment, travel, fashion, and of course gaming itself.

We have access to the winning information and the superstars and legends in the world of gambling, the inside world of Las Vegas, Atlantic City, and other casino destinations, and the pulse of everything that is exciting that you want to read about. We'll keep you coming back with great articles and strategy advice on the games you play (blackjack, craps, slots, video poker, roulette, poker, more!), the sports you follow and bet on (baseball, football, boxing, basketball), and the stranger-than-fiction gambling stories that are just so fascinating, crazy, well, you'll hardly believe it!

Get the confidence Avery Cardoza puts behind every word in print. And get the fun and excitement of the gambling lifestyle—Player Magazine. Go right now to our website—www.cardozaplayer.com—and receive 57% off the subscription price!!!

visit now!!!
www.cardozaplayer.com

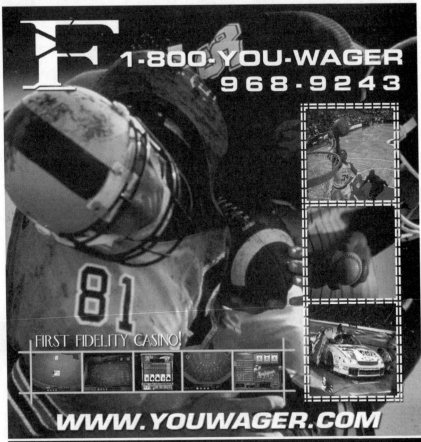